The RecruitMentor

ABOUT THE AUTHOR

After graduating from Queen Mary University of London in 1999, Ross joined one of the UK's most prominent recruitment agencies, quickly becoming an accomplished consultant who would go on to a multi-million career GP.

In 2002, he founded a niche market recruitment company which grew to several £million turnover and counted numerous global brand businesses amongst its customers. Ross sold this business to a multi-national recruitment firm in 2008 and has since freelanced for companies of varying sizes across the UK as a performance training specialist, assessor, and business writer. As of 2016, his work has been used by more than 30 separate platforms and publications.

For more information, please visit
www.therecruitmentor.com

The RecruitMentor
Candidate calls

Ross Owen Williams

The RecruitMentor

First published in 2016 by The RecruitMentor
www.therecruitmentor.com
rw@therecruitmentor.com

British Library Cataloguing in Publication Data
A catalogue record for this book is available from the British Library

ISBN: 978-0-9935420-0-8

This book production has been managed by Amolibros
Printed and bound by Lightning Source

Contents

INTRODUCTION

So, you're looking to make some money in the world of recruitment, eh?

The good news is that there's plenty to be made – and top consultants generally enjoy a great quality of life due to succeeding in recruitment.

These success stories all have one thing in common – an outstanding grasp of the basics.

As complex as it might seem at first, recruitment isn't that tough of a job to do but, all too often, new recruiters are given rudimentary training and told to "get on with it". Learn by doing. Sink or swim.

There's definite value in learning from your mistakes but, if you don't understand how or why you should do something, there's only so far you can go. Making mistakes all of the time without understanding where you're going wrong is frustrating – and frustration can be a career killer.

But if you have a great grasp of the basics and return to them time and time again, you *will* succeed.

That's where this book comes in. The science and art of resourcing in one book, kept simple enough for a newcomer yet something that experienced recruiters can use for a refresher and to make sure they're doing all of the job, all of the time.

I hope you find it useful.

DISCLAIMERS

A few points before we get going...

This is a guide, not a guarantee

This book is full of information that I've picked up over my considerable time in recruitment. I've put this information into practise and it has served me well – I've found jobs for a lot of people and saved time for a lot of businesses. I've taught these lessons to numerous people who have gone on to do extremely well for themselves.

But I can't guarantee that every single point will work *for you*.

Some points, for whatever reason, just don't stick in certain cases. Whilst many of the principles covered herein came quickly to me, there are certainly a few things that took me a considerable number of years to get the hang of. Don't fret, don't panic – just keep working at them. You might get there, you might not. Just keep doing your best.

My writing style

Because I'm a guy, I usually refer to hypothetical people in my writing in the male singular (so a candidate will usually be "he"). Don't infer anything that isn't there – it's simply that using "he/she" all the time is tiresome to write *and* read.

Market discrepancies

Given the book is being written generally, I can't focus on any one recruitment market – as a result, the level of specificity can't be as great as if I wrote strictly about recruiting for only one industry.

However, recruitment is recruitment. Whether you find work for electricians, construction workers or administrators, the principles of the job are the same. Skills, prospects, and geographical and financial expectations will differ from market to market but the resourcer's work always remains to understand the candidate and find a solution to his problem.

Legalities

Each company has its own way of running a business and you've got to play by your company's rules. If there's a discrepancy between what I've written in this book and what you've been told by your employers, by all means raise the issue but, ultimately, what they say goes.

Throughout my books, I touch on legislative matters now and then. I keep these general because legislation is fluid and ever changing – and whilst I've seen a fair few contracts in my time, I'm not a lawyer. If in doubt about legalities, seek advice from the expert at your company because, as a mere wordsmith, I can't take any legal responsibility for your professional actions.

Contingency vs Retained recruitment

A quick definition of the main difference between these two approaches to recruitment, for those who are unclear:

- Retained = fee up front (or some of it, at least)
- Contingency = fee upon placement (no win, no fee)

These books will best benefit those who are working in contingency recruitment and are written with them in mind. This isn't to say that those who work in retained recruitment won't learn a thing or two from *The RecruitMentor* but, generally, people don't get hired for the world of executive search (another term for retained recruitment and somewhat more flattering than "headhunting"!) unless they've already got a damn good grasp of the basics.

Reading tips

Little and often, would be my advice. Much like any form of learning, if you try and take in too much in one sitting, you'll compromise information retention.

Right – now that's all out of the way, let's get started...

RESOURCING – AN OVERVIEW

Resourcing is the task of identifying people who may be worth putting forward to clients (hiring managers at businesses). These potential jobseekers – or candidates – represent a recruiter's "stock", if you will. They are what you will be selling.

Stock your shelves

Imagine you were going to open a clothing business.

You can't simply buy or rent a space, stick up a sign that says "clothes for sale" and expect suits and dresses to magically appear. You've got to stock the shelves yourself (try saying that quickly ten times).

If a potential customer walks into your store and says, "I'm looking for a shirt," you need to be able to point out the shirts you have available rather than saying "Ok, leave it with me, I'll go see what I can find and come back to you in a week or so."

Even getting the potential customer to come into your store in the first place will be tricky unless you've got a display full of enticing wares that makes the punter think "Hmm, that's worth a closer look."

Before you open the doors of your recruitment business to the public, you need stock to sell. You've got to have highly marketable candidates to catch the eye of your customer and show them that your store is worth consideration.

Don't wait for an order

The key to resourcing is to do a little every day – even when you haven't got a job to resource.

But how can you resource if you don't know what your client will need?

Work a niche market

Go back to the clothes shop analogy. If you want a pair of socks, you're in the right place. If you want a wrench, a computer, a treadmill or an ice-cream, you're in the wrong place.

Imagine being a recruiter who works with plumbers in the morning, accountants in the afternoon and IT developers in the evening. You can't put your plumbers forward for accounting positions and you won't get IT developers to trade in their keyboards for a plunger or calculator.

Choose one area of the market and become an expert. Spend all day, every day speaking to people in that market; learn what's going on, who is where and who needs what. Spreading yourself thinly over several different markets will lead to you becoming the proverbial "Jack of all trades and master of none".

Resource generally

Now you've decided to work on one specific market, every candidate you speak to will have some potential use. Some may not be relevant for any of the jobs you have active right now but might be ideal for a vacancy you will find tomorrow.

When speaking to a candidate, don't make your call about a job – make it about the job*seeker*.

Calling about one specific job is grossly time inefficient. All you can learn is whether the candidate will consider the work, location and money on offer at that moment.

What happens when you find another job later with different work, location and money? You have to call the candidate back again to find out how he feels about *that* one too. Not only will you be wasting your time, you'll be wasting his too.

See the big picture

When on an initial resource call, the aim is to get an overview of what makes the candidate tick. What he is doing, why he wants to change his circumstances and what he wants moving forward.

Then, once you know all of these things, you can discuss whether he's a suitable fit for what you have in mind. If he is, great! If he's not, at least you know what he does and doesn't want, so can phone back only when you have something that will work for both of you.

It's simply impossible to call every candidate about every job every time, so you've got to maximise what you get from your initial call.

LOCATING RELEVANT CANDIDATES

Before you pick that phone up, you've got to create a list of people relevant to the sort of jobs that you have (or will have) available.

You won't know for sure until you speak to them but where you find their profile can offer you clues as to their jobseeking state – and it's one of three options:

- **Actively looking** – a candidate unhappy enough with his current situation that he's going out of his way to pursue other jobs.

- **Passively looking** – a candidate open to looking at new opportunities but his current situation is at least tolerable, so he will be more selective in what he goes for.

- **Not looking** – the candidate is perfectly happy with his situation right now thankyouverymuch.

So, let's look at the main places we'll be sourcing candidates from – and which state people from each are most likely to be in.

Company database

Whether your company has been in business for a couple of years or a couple of decades, you'll hopefully have access to a resource pool of legacy candidates who have been spoken to before and/or applied to previous jobs.

Some may have been contacted recently and you'll be able to consider any notes left by your colleagues before making your approach. Others may have not been called in years. Those folks could be looking actively, passively or not looking at all – there's no way of telling from their profile alone.

Advertising

You've put an advert online or in the press, asking people with the skillset you cover to get in touch to discuss your excellent opportunities. Whenever a candidate replies, it's a strong indication he's actively looking for work!

Online CV databases

CVs registered with online databases invite the approach of prospective clients and agents rather than going after any one specific job. These candidates are, in effect, saying "come and get me".

This type of jobseeker could be either actively or passively looking for work.

Also, consider how far back you are searching in the online database. If the candidate registered weeks or months ago, he may already be off the market.

Social media

If you ignore the opportunity of being able to locate and engage with potential candidates through LinkedIn, Twitter, Facebook and the like, you're passing up the chance to substantially increase your candidate network.

Unless a profile indicates otherwise, it's wise to presume the owner is not looking for work – but don't let that stop you politely, discretely offering your services or pitching your vacancy.

After all, nothing ventured, nothing gained.

Personal recommendation

It's always worth considering your own network – this can tie in with the social media point, where you can easily reach a lot of people with minimal effort.

A real life example; just this very morning, I put a status on my Facebook asking if any of my contacts knew anybody with experience of self-publishing. I've since been introduced to FIVE new people with whom to connect.

If you ask to be put in touch with people who are specifically *looking for work*, you limit your results. If you ask to be put in touch with people who work within your field, you'll get a wider selection and then it's up to you to figure out who is actively looking, who is passively looking and who is not looking.

How to search

The ins and outs of how to operate the specific CRM (Customer Relationship Management) systems and online databases that your company uses will be explained by a manager within your organisation but here are a few thoughts to consider...

- When searching skills, start with the narrowest possible criteria. Put *everything* you need into the search field because this will lead you to the best bets first. After all, why call around a list of hundreds of people who are adequate for the job when you can start with the handful of candidates who are, seemingly, ideal?

- Then work backwards – remove one skill or criterion at a time, gradually broadening your search.

- Record the searches you've run and where you've run them – if you don't, you could end up redoing work you've already done.

- Start local and expand from there. It'll be easier for you to sell your job to somebody who lives very close to the location of the work – and it'll be easier for you to sell that candidate to the client.

- Don't search financial boundaries. Some databases allow you to eliminate candidates from your results if the money they say they want doesn't match the money you're able to offer. The reality is that you will usually be able to negotiate candidates down from the financial expectation they've stated online so search for people who seem able to do the job and worry about the money later.

CV SKIMMING

In recruitment, you will hear time and time again that "the phone is your friend", "the phone is king" and "time spent away from the phone is time wasted". Whilst there is some truth to these, there is more truth to the saying that "failing to prepare is preparing to fail".

Cheesy, for sure. But accurate? You betcha.

Before you go ploughing into your resource call, it's important to gather a basic understanding of who you are calling and how to approach this individual – and the key word here is *individual*. If you assume that every candidate is more or less the same, you set yourself up to fail. Many will have similarities but they certainly won't all be the same.

Call preparation is a delicate balancing act – spend too long preparing and you could be wasting your time. Spend too little time preparing and your call may lack focus, miss key points, cover the wrong questions... in short, the call itself could be a waste of time.

How long is too long?

Don't spend more than two minutes reading a CV. You can't guarantee the candidate will answer your call and, if he doesn't, your preparation will have been for nothing. Given the sheer volume of candidates you need to call on any given day, it will be difficult to retain the information gathered during your preparation for whenever a specific candidate gets around to calling you back – and sometimes it's a call that never comes.

What to look for

It's possible to skim read a CV in less than thirty seconds once you know what you're looking for.

- **Location**
  Does the candidate state where he lives? Is there a geographical pattern in his job history? If he has spent his entire life working in the South, starting your pitch with a job up North may be a poor move.

- **Current status**
  Is this guy currently in work? If his employment history suggests he is in a job at present, you know about one of the potential competitors for his services – his current client.

- **Level of seniority**
  There's a big difference between someone with a few years of commercial experience and someone with a

couple of decades – they will likely be at different points in their lives with different needs. They also may expect to be addressed in a different manner. If the person you are speaking to grew up when there were fewer than five billion TV channels, he may expect to be referred to as "Sir" or "Mr." instead of his first name. If in doubt, go with "Mr.", then ask permission to use his first name during the call.

- **Quantity of jobs**
  A large number of jobs in a relatively short amount of time suggests the candidate is a contractor or, alternatively, somebody who cannot/will not stay in any job for long. One is fine, the other less so.

- **Education**
  This can offer a couple of clues. Firstly, you can spot any gaps in the CV. If the candidate finished education ten years ago but his recorded career history began five years ago, is this because he has neglected to give a full work history (and, if so, why?) or did he take five years out before starting work (again, if so, why?). Secondly, if the candidate was educated in a country whose inhabitants can't legally work in yours, this is a red flag – which leads on to…

- **Red flags**
  As well as an international education, you need to see if the candidate has worked in countries which would suggest he might need a work permit to secure a job in yours. The candidate may actually state his nationality

is that of a country which would make it difficult for him to get the legal right to work where you are. Now, we are not going to make assumptions based on these factors but, if any of these red flags are in the CV, they *are* going to factor into our questioning.

- **Referrals**
  Candidates sometimes put the name of a referee or, occasionally, a full testimonial in their CV (most commonly at the very end). Spotting this pre-call will help with lead generation.

- **Interests**
  Some CVs, particularly those of more inexperienced candidates, contain an interests section, usually found at the end of the document. Herein, you'll find a number of subjects that you can use to engage with the jobseeker. More on this later in the book but, before you make a call, have a quick look to see if you share any common interests.

If you've just started in recruitment, you might not think it's possible to absorb all of this information in thirty seconds but, trust me, as you gain experience in skim-reading CVs, you'll dial a number and digest it all whilst the phone is ringing.

I haven't mentioned checking the candidate's skillset and for a simple reason – everybody in your call list should be relevant to your business interests. If they are not, there is something wrong with your initial sourcing process and you need to consider why you are wasting time on candidates who have no use to you.

Whilst some in your call list may turn out to not be ideal for the specific job(s) you are working on *right now*, they *will* have relevance to the market in which you work all day, every day. As mentioned before, candidates who aren't quite right for today's role might be perfect for the tomorrow's vacancy.

Speak to them now and get ahead of the game.

INTRODUCING YOURSELF

How many of us actually get taught how to introduce ourselves? I certainly don't remember being coached on this. As children, some do it naturally, marching up to other kids and saying, "Hi, I'm Steve, let's play." This doesn't seem to work so well as adults.

As a new recruiter, the majority of resource calls you make will be to people who don't know you and phoning a perfect stranger can be intimidating. The person at the other end of the phone might not want to talk. He might hang up. He might yell abuse or report you to your manager for wasting his time. He might report you to the police for bugging him with unsolicited phone calls!

Sure, he *might*.

But he ***won't***.

The worst you'll get is a person saying that he doesn't want to talk and ending the call. No big deal. He's not rejecting you, he's rejecting your approach.

Get to the point with a good, concise introduction. Motivate the candidate to take your phone call and you won't face this issue.

The five elements of a successful introduction

- **Your name**
  Use your full name – it creates a professional first impression. Have you ever had a doctor introduce himself to you as "Dave"? How about a lawyer? Always professional title or full name.

  It's also worth using the most "business sounding" variation of your name. For example, Bobby carries the connotation of boyhood whereas Robert conjures up a more professional image.

- **Your company**
  Whilst the candidate may not have heard of *you*, he may have heard of your company. Announcing, loud and proud, which organisation you represent may lend you credibility in the eyes of the candidate.

  Avoid the "R-word" (recruitment) – you need to break this habit early so you don't instinctively do it on client calls, when it will get you into trouble at switchboard.

- **How you found him**
  The candidate might have been on your database, he might have been on an online CV search site, he might have been referred by a friend – either way, the candidate has a right to know how you have managed to track him down. You are, in effect, answering one of the questions that will be going through his head before he has even asked it.

- **Your history with him**

  One of the first things a candidate will think when you phone him is "Do I know you?" Whilst he's trying to figure this out, he's not actually listening to what you're saying so, rather than ploughing on, take the time to help him understand.

  If this is your first contact, tell him "We've not spoken before..." so the candidate can stop thinking if he knows you and instead focus on what you are about to say.

  If anybody from your company has spoken to the candidate before, point it out. He may recognise your colleague's name and this could prove the common ground that gets the conversation off and running.

- **The reason for the call**

  This is, by far, the most important part of any introduction. If you don't give the candidate a good reason to take your call, he may reject it.

  Yes, you need to find out some information about the candidate but if you phrase it that way, you make the call about what *you* want. The candidate doesn't care about what you want – the candidate is interested in what is in it for *him*.

  Mention that you have a vacancy that you think would suit him or clients who will likely be interested in him. If he is on the market, you can bet your bottom dollar he'll take the call. If he isn't looking, he'll tell you quickly and save you both some time.

How long?

A good introduction will last anywhere between ten to twenty seconds.

If it's taking longer, it'll lose the candidate's interest. If it's shorter, you're probably not giving enough to effectively capture his attention.

Don't overcomplicate it, don't go into depth and don't offer the outline of the job you have in mind. This part of the call is like a game of cards – you don't want to show the other player exactly what you have in your hand but you want him to know that you do at least have *some* cards!

Things to avoid during an introduction...

• *Don't speak like you're calling from a call centre.*

This is liable to have you treated like you *are* calling from a call centre and most people HATE being called by call centre workers.

Constructions such as "My name is..." or "I'm calling from a company called..." just scream for the recipient of the call to hang up and save his time rather than endure a conversation about mis-sold PPI or a customer satisfaction survey.

• *Don't undermine the importance of your call.*

If you tell the candidate that it is "just a quick call" or "will only take a minute", it suggests that what you have to say isn't worth his time, therefore the call is unimportant.

New recruiters tend to do this because they are nervous and don't want to irritate the candidate yet, by starting calls in this way, they actually increase their chances of being seen as annoying.

- *Don't ask if the candidate has time to take your call.*

If you give the candidate the chance to bail out politely, he may well do so.

Being a good recruiter is about staying in control of situations. Letting the candidate dictate when you may speak to him is definitely not staying in control. If the candidate mentions without prompting that it isn't a good time to talk, arrange another time to speak but don't be the one to bring this up – wait for the candidate to mention it first.

- *Don't ask how the candidate is.*

This might seem incredibly rude but, trust me, it's not. In fact, there is little more annoying than somebody you have never spoken to asking you how you are.

If I'm the person getting that call, I don't want to engage in chitchat with a complete stranger, I want to know why you are calling and why it's worth my time taking this call. I'm a busy man – get to the point.

CARROTS

An old adage is that if you want to make a donkey move, you use a carrot to motivate him. Offer a taste and then hold the rest of the carrot in front of him. The donkey, now with carrot on the mind, walks forward hoping to reach – and then devour – the rest of the carrot.

Replace donkey with candidate and carrot with vacancy and you start to see where I'm going. Hopefully. Otherwise I just sound like a crazy person rambling on about donkeys and carrots.

The bottom line is that everything in recruitment comes down to motivation – EVERYTHING.

If you want a candidate to do something for you, you better give him a damn good reason. Don't believe me? Think about why you go to work each day. Do you do it because of the personal gain involved or because your boss is a super nice bloke and you want to help him? It's great to be helpful but there's no shame in acknowledging that, without the personal gain, we wouldn't do it.

And if your boss *is* a super nice bloke, he will totally agree.

RIGHT TO WORK

Legislation regarding the right to work in any given country is changing all of the time so it is important that you know who is legally able to work in your country and who is not. If in doubt, ask your manager what the rules are because they seem to change depending on who is in Government, what their international policy is, what they had for breakfast and whether it's Tuesday or Thursday. Yes, I'm being facetious. Sort of.

Bringing up the right to work should only be done if you have a good reason to believe that a candidate may not be eligible to work in the country. Whilst many won't mind, the occasional candidate may take offence to being asked if he is legally able to work in the country of his birth.

Let's say you are talking to a candidate with a traditional local name, living locally, who has spent his entire career working locally. He might find it irritating to be asked whether he has the right to work locally.

If the person in question has a somewhat more exotic name but everything about him is local, this candidate may think that you are assuming he is *not* eligible to work in the country because of his name. As innocent as such a question might seem to you, some people may consider this borderline racism.

However, if a CV contains any red flags, you are absolutely within your rights to ask this question. In fact, it would be unprofessional of you to *not* ask it.

Not only do you need to ask the question but you need to ask it *early* in the phone call. There is little worse than spending 15 minutes qualifying a candidate only find out that he will need a company to sponsor his work permit. That's 15 minutes of your day that you are not going to get back. If there are red flags in the CV, broach this subject early to avoid the risk of wasting time.

Don't pussyfoot around the subject. If you're going to ask, just ask. It will help your cause if you explain why you are asking – for example, if you're recruiting for a job in the UK and the candidate's CV says that he is a national of a non-EU country, simply ask "I see you were born outside the EU; do you have the right to work in Britain?"

The more you drag out the question, the more awkward it will get. The less confident you are in asking it, the more embarrassing it will be for everybody. Get it over and done with.

If the candidate does *not* have the relevant work permits and your company doesn't generally deal with such cases (most recruitment companies won't), politely but firmly explain that neither you nor your client sponsor work visas so there is nothing you can do. The candidate may protest. He may try and make you feel guilty, he may accuse you of trying to prevent him working – ignore him.

It is not your business to say who does and doesn't have the right to work in the country. If the candidate wants to kick up a stink about it, he needs to start with local politicians, not you.

"I'M NOT LOOKING"

It's very tempting to beat a hasty retreat as soon as we hear those words. After all, if the candidate isn't on the market, we're just wasting our time on the phone to him, right?

Not necessarily.

There are two types of "not looking" people.

Those who aren't looking.

And those who aren't looking "unless..."

Ask the candidate under what circumstances it would be worth you getting in touch. Even if he's happy in his current position, surely he wants to hear about any jobs that would double his income? Surely he wants to hear about any jobs that would halve his daily commute? Surely he wants to hear about any jobs which will see him shoot up the corporate ladder?

Make it an offer the candidate can't refuse and, generally, he won't refuse.

That said, some people will still say "no thanks" and reiterate that they're happy where they are. That's perfectly fine. No point banging your head against a brick wall. Find out where they are (so you can catch them further down the line if needs be) and how long they will be off the market (contract finish date or estimate of how long they'll be content in a perm job), see if you can get a candidate referral (covered in the *Lead Generation* section of this book) and move on with your day.

But if the candidate IS interested in being kept informed about certain things – no matter how seemingly unrealistic – you've converted a NOT looking guy to a PASSIVELY looking guy.

On paper, he won't look like a great bet because he's got no real reason to change his current situation unless you find him something better. There's a positive to be found in that though – because he's not actively looking, many other recruiters will simply pass him by, so there won't be as much competition for the passive jobseeker as there is for somebody actively applying for every relevant job he sees.

Providing you actually can find the passive jobseeker something better than what he's got right now, you've got a decent shot at making a placement. But before you get that far, you've got to understand his current situation.

A passive jobseeker's motivation is *always* "to get something better than what I've got" – a very limited motivation and quite different to the range of reasons an active jobseeker seeks to change his circumstances. Your job with this potential candidate is to find out what constitutes "better" – because making assumptions here can be disastrous.

JOBSEEKING MOTIVATION

Everything in recruitment comes down to motivation. This extends to understanding why the candidate you are speaking to is looking for a new job.

Some people don't need to work

If the person in question isn't currently in work, it is tempting to assume that his motivation for taking a job is simply because he doesn't currently have one. In most cases, this may well prove accurate. However, it is still important to understand why that candidate *needs* a job.

Don't paint them with your own perception of the world – many younger recruiters make the assumption that everybody needs a job because, in their comparatively limited life experience, they have always needed a job.

This may ring true of candidates in their twenties and thirties but once you start dealing with more senior candidates, you are more likely to come across people who have sufficient savings to not have to rush back into work.

If your candidate is not currently in work, establish whether or not he is looking for a job due to financial necessity. A candidate who can cope financially for a while will be more selective in his job search than somebody who has looming bills and no money to pay them with.

The end is near

Some candidates are in work but know that the well is going to run dry soon.

Whether a candidate is in a permanent job and has been given notice or is in a temporary assignment that is finishing soon, he will be without work in a finite period of time and, therefore, should be considered in the same category as somebody who is not presently working because neither can see where next months' paycheque is coming from – but they can both probably see some bills on the horizon.

Understand the PAIN

If the candidate is currently in secure work with no finish date in sight, it is vital to find out why he wants to move on. After all, he has a job – why does he need a new one? There must be something that he is *not* getting from his current work situation that is important to him.

This is the PAIN (always capitals!).

In order to understand the candidate, you must understand his PAIN. In order to give him a solution, you must understand what his problem is.

A foolish recruiter simply says "this candidate is looking for a new job and that's good enough for me". People don't look for new jobs "just because". If anything, most human beings are resistant to change so it usually takes something pretty serious to get a person to resign from his job.

It is vital that you do not offer the candidate multiple choice when it comes to his jobseeking motivation. Explore the subject using open questions and *never* accept the first answer. If you use closed questions and make assumptions as to why the candidate is looking for a new job, you may only find out half the story.

Many new recruiters make the assumption that the only reasons a person would want a new job are career progression, an easier commute, more money or more interesting work. Whilst these are the most common reasons for switching a job, they are not the *only* reasons. Even when they do turn out to be true, there is more to be discovered within each subject.

- *"I want more money"*

The key here is find out what he is currently making and what he believes he is worth. Once you know this, you can find out why the candidate feels he is worth the extra money and why his current client seems to disagree.

It's also important to understand why the candidate wants a pay increase – rather than just taking the line of "everybody wants more money", it's worth finding out whether it is a need or want. A candidate who needs to earn more because he is going through a divorce and has maintenance to pay for his children and the upkeep of two households is a different candidate to somebody who is coping fine on what he is being paid right now and just fancies having a bit more in the bank each month.

- *"I want an easier commute"*

How long is the current commute taking? What method is he using to do it? What impact is the current commute having on his life in general?

Above all else, if the commute is troublesome, why did he accept the job in the first place? You may find there has been a change in circumstances that has made a formerly tolerable commute now intolerable.

- *"I want more interesting work"*

Has the work always been boring or has it only recently become so? Has the candidate's skillset increased but his level of responsibility remained static? What exactly is it that the candidate is finding uninspiring about his day-to-day duties?

- *"I want career progression"*

Why is the candidate not able to achieve this in his current company? Why is he being overlooked for promotion? Why does he feel he deserves this career progression and why does he need it now?

Pushing each point will help you construct an accurate picture of the problem you have to solve in order to get the candidate out of his current job and into yours. If you simply accept the first answer, you find out the reason but not the impact – and the impact is what causes people to make changes.

Other reasons a person might decide to switch jobs include (but are not limited to) disliking his boss, disliking his colleagues, not enjoying the social scene within his company, feeling the office environment "isn't right", that the hours are too long, the company isn't flexible when it comes to working arrangements, the benefits package is underwhelming, the expectation to work from home outside of core hours is overwhelming... I even had somebody once resign because the job (a standard trainee recruitment role) was "interfering with (her) sex life". Seriously. You never know what is going to break a worker's will!

And then you have the iconic reason for leaving almost invariably used at least once by anybody under the age of 25...

"It's not my fault, it's theirs"

If the candidate you are speaking to goes into a big song and dance about how nasty and evil his existing employer is, the chances are that he will find something to dislike with any job that you put him in. Until the candidate matures enough to realise that it is more productive to look in the mirror than to point the finger, he is best avoided.

So, as you can see, there are a plethora of reasons why a person might be looking for a new job – identify this in each of your candidates and you not only have the means by which to judge how serious they are about jobseeking and how realistic they are as a jobseeker but you also have something to sell back to them.

If you know that a candidate is unhappy with his current commute because it is preventing him getting home in time to read his kids a bedtime story, you can point out throughout the recruitment process that if he accepts your job, he will quickly be back to reading little Jimmy a chapter of the BFG every night.

That, dear reader, will go a lot further than "take my job because I want the commission for myself".

CURRENT SITUATION – OVERVIEW

The thing most likely to stop a candidate switching jobs is his current position.

And yet some recruiters don't bother discussing the candidate's current job in any detail. They focus strictly on the job that they want the candidate to take and not on what the candidate will be leaving behind.

If you don't understand what your candidate is currently doing, how is it possible to find him something "better"?

The answer is simple – you can't.

If you're not finding out what the candidate is currently doing, you're trading on hope – hope that the job you offer will weigh up favourably against the job he currently has. You might get lucky but luck doesn't make a top consultant.

Never talk about the future unless you know what the candidate is doing right now – it's like pulling the trigger on a gun without having any idea where the target is. You've got to know what you're aiming for before you take a shot.

CURRENT SITUATION – STATUS

You need to find out whether your candidate is in permanent or temporary work. There are numerous words used to denote the latter, from interim to contract to temp, but it all boils down to a finite period of work which has a natural end date and is, therefore, different to permanent work.

Don't assume that you can glean this information from a CV – some permanent jobs end up only lasting for a handful of months and it is not uncommon for contracts to extend year after year.

It is also tempting to assume that the work is full-time. In the majority of cases, it will be. However, a great recruiter trades on facts.

Consider this – who is earning more, a candidate who earns £30 per hour (ph) or a candidate who earns £40ph? The answer is the guy who is earning £30ph… because he gets forty hours each week and the other guy only gets twenty.

Game changer.

CURRENT SITUATION – LOCATION

The CV should contain the name of the company where the candidate is currently working (and if it doesn't, ask. You have a right to know... and so does your client and his potential next boss!) but you also need to know the geographical location.

Don't assume you'll be able to find the location by looking on the web. Many companies have more than one site or registered office. By not asking, you could create more work for yourself later.

Find out how far the candidate's workplace is from his home AND the method he uses to commute.

Finding out the method of commute is important – imagine a candidate says he is commuting thirty minutes each way each day. You might be tempted to think that your job is a better bet because he'll be able to drive door-to-door in twenty minutes but if you knew his twenty minute commute is actually a twenty minute *walk* which, if needs be, he can drive in three minutes, it would change things entirely, wouldn't it?

It's also worth finding out if his existing client offers any opportunity to work from home. A person who works from home two days a week is a very different candidate than somebody who has to commute to and from the office Monday through Friday.

CURRENT SITUATION – AVAILABILITY

Unless you know how long it will take for your candidate to cease working for his existing client, you don't know how soon he could potentially start for a new client, so it's vital you discuss his notice period.

Official notice period

There will be a specific length of time mentioned in the candidate's contract that he needs to offer his existing client in order to wrap up his term of work. This will vary depending on the seniority of the candidate, the responsibility level of his job and the length of service.

Don't assume, don't ask closed questions and don't give multiple choices – keep it to a simple, open question of, "What is your notice period?" I've seen people with as much as six months' notice and I've seen others who only need to give their client a single day's notice. You won't know until you ask.

Negotiated notice period

Many clients don't hold their workers to the length of notice stipulated in their contract. In some cases, the client will welcome the opportunity to release the worker sooner because it will save money and reduce potential negative impact on office morale.

It is always worth asking your candidate what he feels he could negotiate his existing client down to in terms of a reduced notice period.

No notice period

If you're talking about reducing the notice period, you might as well take it all the way and enquire how the candidate would feel about leaving his current job *without* giving notice.

If your client needs somebody to start a job immediately and you know an ideal fit, you need to know if the candidate is prepared to miss out because of his notice period. If the candidate's jobseeking motivation is strong enough and the new position is an opportunity that solves his PAIN, he may well be willing to burn a bridge with his existing client.

You certainly shouldn't encourage a candidate to take this drastic measure but it's worth gently mentioning and gauging the candidate's reaction.

Finish date

Although most permanent employees won't have a finish date until they actually hand in their notice (an exception being permanent workers who are being made redundant), a temporary worker will be able to tell you when his existing contract expires. Some might say that this is irrelevant because a contract is only as long as the notice period but to not know when a contract naturally expires is foolish.

Take a person who has six months left on his existing term of work and compare him to another candidate who has only six weeks left. One of them is getting a paycheque in eight weeks time and the other is not – they are going to react differently to your approach and are likely to have different levels of urgency in their jobseeking. The likelihood is that the candidate with six months left on his contract can afford to be picky and only accept an 8/10 job (or better) whilst, if he needs the work, the candidate with only six weeks work remaining will probably accept the first 6/10 job he gets offered.

CURRENT SITUATION – MONEY

You need to find out what your candidate is currently being paid or you won't have any template for comparison in terms of what he wants moving forward. If you know that your candidate is looking for £40,000 a year in his next job, that's one thing. If you know that he is currently making only £30,000 per year, that puts a whole new angle on this person as a jobseeker. If somebody asked me for a 33% pay increase, I'd damn sure have some questions…

Benefits

Most permanent employees will be offered a benefits package as part of their remuneration. This is not money per se but it can be valuable and is something that a candidate will have to leave behind if he leaves his current job so it's vital for you to know about. After all, a candidate earning £30,000 a year with no bonuses and no benefits package is very different to a candidate earning £30,000 a year with a 10% annual bonus, life insurance, health insurance, pension, subsidised gym membership and flexitime.

Extras

Similarly, the perks and pleasantries of a job can be difficult to leave behind. Whether it's that the client's office has free parking (which, when you consider the scandalous cost of parking these days, can make a huge difference) or simply that the candidate is working with three of his best friends, these are things that could cause a candidate to reject your job and stay where he is.

By the way, a key difference benefits and extras are that benefits are generally taxable whilst extras aren't.

Not just for permies...

A note to any contract recruiters reading this – just because contractors don't get benefits, it doesn't mean there aren't perks and pleasantries to be considered as well. Identify what your candidate will find it hard to leave behind in his current job and you will be working from a much better brief.

JOBSEEKING PREFERENCES –
OVERVIEW

Now you understand the current circumstances of a candidate, you have a template for comparison and an idea of what the candidate is likely to want moving forward so, if any of his jobseeking preferences surprise you, you can discuss the discrepancy.

For example, if you find a candidate who says he'll commute no more than 15 minutes each way yet you now know he's doing an hour each way each day, you'll be more likely to attempt to persuade the candidate to expand his parameters. 45 minutes might not be ideal but at least it's better than an hour!

Don't lead the candidate to the answer

Although you should have a reasonable idea of what the candidate is likely to want, you mustn't assume.

If you use constructions like, "I don't suppose you want to commute any further than you currently are?" or, "you'll be looking for a higher rate in the next job, won't you?" the candidate will likely just say "sure" and you'll delude yourself into thinking that you're doing your job. What you're *actually* doing is creating problems by assuming and not fact finding.

Keep your questions open – that way, you encourage the candidate to tell you what he genuinely thinks rather than confirming or denying your assumptions. Once he's opened the proverbial bidding, you can push up or down as necessary and find out what is ideal, what is acceptable, and where the candidate will draw the line and say no.

JOBSEEKING PREFERENCES – STATUS

Is the candidate looking for contract or permanent? Full-time or part-time work?

To assume that he wants a full-time permanent job because "people need stability" is a rookie mistake. Believe it or not, there can be more stability in a contract role than there in permanent employment. I've known contractors who've worked with the same company for in excess of five years and I've known permies who've flown the coop in a matter of months.

Take off the blinkers

It's tempting to speak to a candidate only about the sort of vacancy, perm or contract, that *you* cover. Just because *you* may be limited to operating in only one area of the market, it doesn't mean the candidate is under that same obligation.

A person with ten years' experience and only two jobs on his CV, both permanent positions, might well look like a great prospect for full-time employment but *he* might think he now has enough experience to become a highly-paid freelance consultant. If you were to assume that this candidate is *only* interested in permanent work, you would be working from a faulty brief.

Similarly, how about the individual who has worked for numerous companies as a freelancer? To assume that he wants to continue contracting is to invite disaster. He might have recently started a family and decided that the uncertainty of contract work is not conducive to his new responsibilities as a parent. He'll listen to contract offers but what he really wants now is the (apparent) stability of full-time employment.

In these situations, a recruiter who makes assumptions may spend his time thinking he is working with a excellent candidate – only to find that he's been offering the candidate what amounts to a worst-case scenario job.

Understand preference

If you've established your candidate is open to both types of work, ask about his preference. If he has two comparable offers, one permanent and one contract, which would he be more likely to take? You need to get a feel for how serious a prospect the candidate is for you. How much of your time do you want to commit to somebody who won't commit to doing what you do?

JOBSEEKING PREFERENCES – LOCATION

Where does he live?

After your initial questioning, you should know where your candidate lives – now, it's important to dig a little deeper and understand what he's near to because that will have an impact on your chances of placing him.

How close he is to key commuting points such as a motorway junction or a train station? Somebody who lives in a small town but right next to the train station may well be a better prospect than somebody living in a city but in a very difficult place to commute from.

Length of commute?

Keep it simple and keep it uniform – decide whether you're going to ask how far candidates are willing to commute in miles or in minutes. Both can sometimes be misleading but people generally have a better idea of what half an hour is than, say, twenty miles, so I'd suggest sticking to the time approach.

Flex!

If the candidate is willing to commute half an hour each way, try for 45 minutes. If he is willing to consider *that*, push to an hour.

Keep pushing up until there is resistance.

The more you expand his geographical search, the more options you will be able to offer. Help the candidate see this and you'll get his genuine top line.

Flex more!

Don't discount the possibility that your candidate may be willing to relocate or work away from home.

Some candidates may have deep roots where they live but others may be open to working further afield. Some contractors are happy to live away from home from Monday to Friday or "weekly commute", so if your job is appealing, a contractor might agree to work for a company nowhere near where he lives.

Working away from home is not reserved exclusively for contractors – some permanent jobseekers may have had changes in personal circumstances that allow them to move to wherever an appealing job is. Some candidates might welcome such a major change. Whether it be a younger jobseeker looking to get away from the area in which he has grown up or an older jobseeker who has, say, been through a divorce and is looking to start afresh in a new part of the country, you won't know whether your candidate is open to the idea of relocation unless you ask.

JOBSEEKING PREFERENCES – AVAILABILITY

"Hang on a minute..." I hear you cry. "We've covered this already!"

No, we haven't. We've covered availability in terms of being able to leave an existing job, not availability to start a future job. You simply can't presume that your candidate will start a new job immediately after finishing his existing job.

Time off

Your candidate might want a week off between jobs. Perhaps he wants to spend some time with his family. Perhaps he wants to take care of a couple of long-neglected things around the house. Perhaps he has been fed up in his job for so long that he simply wants a week's holiday to recharge before he gets his nose back to the grindstone. Whatever the reason, this sort of situation is a game changer because, suddenly, a candidate with a four week notice period becomes somebody who is available five weeks after handing in his notice.

More time off

Some candidates want more than a week between jobs. Some want a fortnight. Some might insist on a month. Some may go even further – I had a contractor once tell me that he was intending to take THREE MONTHS off between jobs.

It turns out that his daughter was getting married and he was intending to use the summer to oversee all the arrangements, as well as project managing an extension for his home. If I had presumed he was going to start a new contract as soon as his existing job finished, I would have wasted my time and looked rather foolish to my clients.

As I did in another situation – this was how I learned my lesson about the difference between finish date and start date.

Having had several candidates go through the interview process with a major credit checking company, I was delighted to receive three offers for candidates I had put forward. Phoning the first of them to tell her the good news, I gleefully reported that she could hand in her notice and, when that four-week period had expired, she would start her new job with my client.

"No, I won't," she said.

I was stumped. All I could manage to mutter was, "But… why?"

Then she dropped the bombshell. "Because I've got a three-week holiday booked."

"You didn't tell me," I stammered – to which she very rightly responded, "You didn't ask."

Egg on face, I phoned the client back to explain that this particular candidate would not be able to take up the job for seven weeks. The client understandably rescinded the offer and gave the job to somebody else. Not only had I wasted my time but I had also made myself look less than competent in front of a paying customer.

Yes, this candidate could – and probably should – have told me about this lengthy impending holiday but, as the manager of the recruitment process, it is the recruiter's responsibility to cover all of the bases. As vital a point as a three week delay might seem to you or I, some candidates will not think to offer information like this unless they are specifically asked about it.

Remain in control of the situation and find out the exact timescales that you will be working to.

JOBSEEKING PREFERENCES – MONEY

One of the more asinine questions I've been asked by recruiters is "what is your ideal rate?"

The answer is pretty obvious. As much as I can get!

Let's face facts – when it comes to financial expectations, nobody is going to start low and then attempt to haggle up. Your candidate will tell you what he WANTS and it is your job to find out what he will accept and when he will say NO.

Start with the dream

Once you've found out what the candidate is after, assure him you will do your best but then explore what will happen if you offer less. You'll usually find that a candidate will readily admit that he will consider jobs for slightly less money (around 5% less) but to push somebody down further requires a firm hand.

Work backwards to reality

Once you have got your candidate down to what he claims is his bare minimum, use the construction known as the "takeaway close".

If the candidate claims he is not interested in any job paying less than £40,000 per year, say that you won't call about any jobs that pay £39,000, no matter how exciting or local they might be.

Some candidates will be fine with this but others will suddenly backtrack. "Well, if it's only a *little* bit less, we could talk about it…"

This leads to further conversation where you establish the candidate's *genuine* bottom-line, the figure beneath which you shouldn't even consider getting in touch.

Withholding information

Some candidates are unwilling to disclose their genuine bottom-line because they believe the recruiter will then only ever offer their bare minimum.

A good recruiter understands that it is far more profitable in the long term to keep a candidate happy than it is to force him to accept a rate that is a borderline "no".

A candidate who is unhappy with what he is being paid is more likely to leave a job. If your candidate quits, you lose credibility with the person who pays your fees – the client. The more you can do to keep your candidate happy, the more likely it is that he will stay put – and the more likely it is that you will continue to make placements with your happy client.

Convince your candidates

Permanent recruiters have a very easy time in convincing their candidates that they will push to get the best salary – because they (usually) work on a fixed percentage fee with the client, the more money they get for their candidate, the more money they get for themselves. It is in the interest of the recruiter to get the candidate as much as possible without making the client feel like he has overpaid.

On contract, it is less precise. Recruiters tend to work to an unspecified margin, charging the client one figure, paying the candidate another and keeping the difference.

Some recruiters use this as an opportunity to try and take as much as possible – a foolish move because if either the candidate or the client discovers what the discrepancy is (and, usually, they will because they *do* talk – and don't kid yourself otherwise!) and deems it unfair, you may not just lose this contract but you may lose both the candidate's trust *and* all future business with that client. It's just not worth the risk. A good, productive, long-term business relationship is worth far more than a quick hit, maximum profit deal.

The best way to allay the fears of a contractor is to explain that it is in your interests to get him as much as possible because a well-paid contractor is a happy contractor. The more you can pay, the more likely he is to extend his contract and give his best to that client. The more you pay, the more likely he is to recommend you to his peers.

The bottom line

Whether working on permanent or contract, the key is to explain that you are trying to find out about the absolute bottom line not to better line your own pockets but because you don't want to mistakenly turn viable opportunities away.

Once the candidate understands that getting the best deal for him is in your best interests, he'll discuss the matter of money much more openly.

DELIVERY AND TEST

By now, you should understand

- What the candidate is currently doing
- Why he wants to change his circumstances
- What he wants to change them to

You've taken a lot of information from him so it's time to give something back.

Remember the analogy about the donkey and the carrot? Now it's time to deliver the carrot. You promised to discuss some jobs that might be suitable for him, so pony up… or donkey up, I guess.

Discuss an appropriate job

Given what you've learned about the candidate, you should be able to weigh what he will and won't do against your current vacancies and discuss anything appropriate.

Don't go into huge detail – you don't have the time to read every job spec to him. Tell him about the money, the location and the general skills needed. If they fit his criteria, tell him you'll send his CV to the client and leave it at that. If the client has given you specific questions to ask, ask them. Otherwise, you should be able to deduce whether the candidate is suitable or not by looking at his CV, considering his jobseeking motivation and parameters. Beyond that, it's the client's decision.

If the client is interested in pursuing the candidate, *then* you can call back and go into the minute details of the job. Until then, you could be wasting time by reading a long job description to a candidate who will then say either "ok" or "no thanks". If you spend one minute reading full job specs to every candidate every day, that could be upwards of half an hour that you could use to do something more productive.

What if you haven't got anything appropriate?

If you haven't got any roles that might fit the bill, you have two options;

- *Tell him you've got nothing for him.*

Put yourself in the shoes of the candidate – he's just taken ten minutes of his time to talk you through his current situation and what he's after, only to have you deliver the crushing blow of "I've got nothing." Sure, you'll say that you'll keep looking for him but that's little consolation.

The candidate needs something more than this – and you should deliver it.

- *Tell him you know some clients who might be interested.*

Because, as an expert recruiter (or an aspiring one), you *should* know some clients who might be interested. Even if you don't, your colleagues might. You *should* be able to find something on the company database to fit the bill. With a little effort, even if you don't have an active vacancy, you *should* be able to put his CV in front of somebody who uses his skills and is within his commute parameters.

Reiterate this to the candidate.

If he's an electrician looking for work within thirty minutes of home, tell him that you'll get in touch with several companies you know who use electricians and are based within thirty minutes of his home. It's a lot better than saying "I've got nothing, sorry." Providing you don't make false promises (e.g. "I'll call you back with an interview."), it's better for a candidate to leave the call with *some* hope rather than no hope.

And if you are a good recruiter, you *will* get in touch with those companies to see whether they can use this excellent candidate. It's called basic pitching!

Better still...

The wise recruiter can use job delivery as a way of testing the information that has just been acquired.

Sure, it's easy to tell the candidate about one or two jobs that tick all of his boxes but what do you learn from that? Using the delivery to simply placate the candidate and offer him a "yes" job is to miss a golden opportunity.

Discuss a couple of "no" jobs instead.

Not outlandish "no way in hell" jobs but "only just no" jobs.

Tell him about a client based *just beyond* his maximum commute radius.

Tell him about another client looking to pay *just beneath* the minimum level of money he expects.

He *should* say no to both.

If he does, excellent. It means that he has been genuine with you in his geographical and fiscal requirements.

If, however, he says he would like to be put forward to either of these "no" jobs, you *haven't* found out his genuine parameters. This then gives you the chance to revisit the topic and get a proper grasp of his requirements.

If you decide to leave the call after having offered him a "no" job that he has, in fact, said no to, it need not be seen as negative. Emotionally, it's better that he rejects your offer than you reject him. You've offered him an opportunity and it was *his* decision to not be put forward. He will feel less like he has wasted his time than if you simply said, "Ok, I've got nothing for you but I'll be in touch."

LEAD GENERATION – OVERVIEW

Every call to a candidate gives you the opportunity to learn more about the market in which you work. Often, you will pick up information purely by accident as one candidate might tell you about a new project he is working on and another might mention a technology that is due to be released imminently.

Lead generation, however, is about *actively* acquiring market information (or MI) which you can use to place more business.

Before we get into an explanation of the various types of leads, what they can do for you and how to get them, I want to discuss the overall subject of lead generation, especially the perception of some who don't understand the recruitment industry.

The big picture

Some people consider lead generation to be the recruitment equivalent of insider trading – something underhanded and purely done for the benefit of the individual acquiring the information.

This is untrue.

There is nothing wrong with acquiring information wherever you can providing the information is given willingly and you are not breaking any laws in doing so. If you were forcing candidates to give you information under duress, I could see a problem. However, asking for information and giving a good reason for the candidate to freely offer it? I'm not sure many could find fault in that.

Yes, we are going to get information about former employers and future clients from the candidates we speak to but, done correctly, this is not to the detriment of the person divulging the information.

The fear

Protesters will claim that, if a candidate tells you where he had an interview last week, you will try to "steal" that job. If he tells you the name of a previous employer, you will hound that individual and mar the relationship between candidate and former boss. Due to these preconceptions (which have, regrettably, been fed by the behaviour of lesser and, no doubt, now-former recruiters), some candidates can be rather stubborn when it comes to discussing such things.

These candidates are, unfortunately, being rather short-sighted.

All they can see is what they might lose rather than considering what they might gain. By sharing information with a good, reliable recruiter, they could benefit hugely. There isn't an industry on this planet where knowledge-sharing between professionals doesn't lead to positive results.

The more you build up a good reputation for professionalism, hard work and commitment to quality service, the more you will develop relationships with people who will trust you to do the right thing with the information they provide.

An example

Let's say that you speak to 25 candidates each day. If you work within one specific market (as you should!), they will all be of a similar background so that the work you do for one is relevant for all.

If one candidate gives you the name of a hiring manager, you can potentially use that information for the benefit of the other 24 candidates you will speak to that day, not to mention the countless other candidates you will speak to over the subsequent week, month, year and beyond.

In exchange for giving you this information, that one candidate will benefit from the information you are given by the other 24 candidates you speak to that day. That seems like a fair trade to me.

Don't get me wrong – I understand why people are sometimes reticent to do this with recruiters they don't yet trust. In the hands of an amoral recruiter, this sort of information can be used selfishly and thoughtlessly. However, recruiters who act in such a fashion will quickly gain a negative reputation, generate complaints to higher-ups within their company and, ultimately, be victims of their own avarice.

Integrity is invaluable

My personal view on lead generation is the same now as it was when I started in recruitment way back in the middle of the 17th century (or so it seems).

I have to be able to look myself in the mirror.

If I have deprived somebody of something for my own personal gain, that makes me no more than a thief.

If, on the other hand, I have acquired information that is useless to one individual in order to help another, I'm more than entitled to give my reflection a nod of approval.

VERBAL REFERENCE LEADS

What are they?

A verbal reference lead consists of:

- The name of a candidate's former manager
- The company at which he worked
- The location of the business

What's in it for you?

Let's say that you are speaking to a candidate because he is a copywriter. All of his jobs have been copywriting jobs. The reason his former clients hired him is because of his copywriting skills (and, if in doubt, the candidate's CV will indicate what he did at any given company).

Therefore, if you are the sort of recruiter who finds work for copywriters, it is highly likely that any of this candidate's former clients will hire the sort of people that you provide. Speaking to clients like this is a far better use of your time than phoning up any old company and hoping for the best.

It's better for the client too – phone calls offering him things that he can use is far preferable to phone calls offering him services that he can't.

What's in it for the candidate?

Firstly, it gives you the chance to establish the candidate's quality with somebody who has spent money on his services. Once he's been vouched for, you will work harder to place him in a job.

Secondly, in the same way that this candidate's verbal reference may help your other candidates, other verbal references will benefit the original candidate. By willingly helping you expand your network, he stands to be one of the primary beneficiaries.

How can you get this information?

- *The full explanation*

As much as I generally believe "honesty is the best policy", going over everything outlined in the previous section is inadvisable.

You haven't got the time to explain everything to every candidate, so save the full-length explanation only for those who really need it. Also, the more you explain to a candidate, the more chance there is that he will find something objectionable – so don't make this process unnecessarily overcomplicated.

- *The selfish approach*

Tell the candidate that you want to do business with his former client.

In this approach, the candidate stands to gain nothing and you stand to gain everything – so you'd better make it worth his while. Motivate him by saying that when you place any business with somebody to whom he introduces you, you will pay him a referral fee.

(And if you *do* place with that client, make sure you cough up the fee and don't make him chase you to get it. Some recruiters "forget" in order to keep the money and hope the candidate doesn't find out. That's odd, since delivering what you promised will strengthen your relationship with the candidate and make him more likely to help you in the future!)

- *The selfless approach*

Explain how much a good verbal reference can do for the candidate.

People prefer to buy a car with a full service history because it suggests the buyer is going to get a quality product. It's the same with references – if two comparably skilled people are put forward for a job, do you think the client will go with the candidate who has three excellent verbal references or the candidate who refuses to give the names of his former managers?

- *The compulsory approach*

To ensure they are dealing with vetted individuals, some clients insist on verbal references.

Some companies even insist on recruiters submitting shortlists via an online portal, complete with various information fields to fill in – with one of these being for references so, unless this can be completed, the application won't go through.

If the candidate wants to be in the running for the job, he needs to conform with the client's request.

INTERVIEW LEADS

What are they?

A basic interview lead requires:

- The name of the company looking to hire
- The site at which the job is based

Anything beyond this is a bonus but you can make the best possible approach to the best possible person if you also find out:

- The name of the interviewing manager
- What sort of job it is (contract/perm)
- The level of money on offer
- The process progress (first interview, second interview, offer rejected etc.)
- How recently the interview happened

What's in it for you?

You will be able to go directly to the later stages of the recruitment process, skipping the need to make countless canvass calls in order to find somebody who has a vacancy.

Do be aware, however, that because interviews have already begun, joining a process at this late stage can be like starting to run the 100m when your competitors are already 50m down the track!

What's in it for the candidate?

It depends what stage the recruitment process it at.

If he's still in play, by telling an agent about what he's got lined up, he could increase the competition for the job (if the agent is one of those stab-you-in-the-back types). Perhaps the candidate will benefit from information gleaned from other candidates in return for talking about his own interviews but there's no guarantee.

However, if the candidate has either been rejected from the process or turned down an offer, he has nothing to lose by offering up this information and could gain a referral fee if you can place the job.

How can you get this information?

• *The business approach*

Ask the candidate outright if he has turned down any offers or been rejected after interview by any companies.

He will probably ask why you want to know.

Explain that, since he didn't get the job, there is surely no harm in you seeing if another of your candidates might well be a better fit for that vacancy. Incentivise him by offering a referral fee should you place a vacancy.

If the candidate feels there is still a chance of him getting this job, it's inadvisable to put your cards on the table about wanting to submit some of *your* candidates. Even though most recruiters would agree that a candidate who hasn't heard anything from the client after a week is clearly not going to get the job, some candidates will convince themselves they are still in with a chance.

- *The avoidance approach*

Tell the candidate that you want to be proactive and get his profile in front of as many relevant hiring managers as possible – after all, this is what a good recruiter does.

But if you don't know where he has interviewed, you can't avoid that particular company. You definitely don't want to replicate his details because it will make you look unprofessional and, worse still, will make the candidate look desperate – which may affect his chances of getting the best deal possible.

These are fair and realistic points. However, problems arise when they are delivered by recruiters who have no intention of actually marketing the candidate and are simply spinning a line to extract information under false pretences. Don't be one of them!

Regarding timescales

Always try to find out when the interview happened. It has an impact on what happens next.

If you find out that an interview happened some time ago, it is fair to presume the candidate has not been successful and a gentle approach to the client is not unreasonable.

If you find out that the interview has happened fairly recently, the candidate still may be in the running. This then becomes a grey area. Some might say that, upon approach, the only reason a client would use your services would be if he is not satisfied with the people he has seen so far.

If you find out about an interview that hasn't happened yet, you can approach the client, interest him in one of your candidates and potentially close the deal before the guy who told you about the vacancy has even had a chance to interview.

This is far less of a grey area – it's not on.

This is a clear case of depriving somebody of an opportunity. It's one thing if a candidate has an interview and blows it but it's quite another for you to steal the opportunity from him.

Any recruiter who believes this sort of practice is acceptable is doing the industry a huge disservice.

APPLICATION LEADS

What are they?

An application lead requires:

- The name of the company where a candidate's CV has been sent
- The location of the company (if it is known)

As with interview leads, any extra information about type of work, money on offer and the like is useful but not vital to tracking down the vacancy (if the vacancy actually does exist... more on this in a moment!).

In short, an application lead is when a candidate has been told he has been put forward for a job but has not yet been offered an interview.

This could be due to any one of four things:

- The vacancy *is* real but the candidate doesn't/didn't make the interview shortlist

- The vacancy *is* real and the client hasn't got around to arranging interviews yet (and there is no guarantee that the candidate will get an interview even then)

- The vacancy *is* real but the recruiter didn't submit the candidate's CV, despite saying he would

- The vacancy *isn't* real and the recruiter was lying to win favour with the candidate

Do some recruiters really tell candidates that they will put them forward to a specific company simply to win their favour? You'd better believe it. Who are you more likely to give your time to? The recruiter who doesn't have anything for you or the recruiter who seems keen to put you forward to Microsoft or Mercedes or a similar household name?

Now, before you go telling everybody that you will put them forward to companies like that in order to easily acquire information, consider this – you have to deliver at some point. "But they can't prove I *didn't* put them forward..." you say. Correct – but the more you say you'll do something with no visible result, the less credibility you'll have. Do it enough and nobody will believe a word you say. Don't get on that slippery slope because somebody will realise you're making false promises and it will come back to haunt you.

What's in it for you?

It could either be a decent lead or a complete waste of your time.

If the vacancy never existed in the first place, you will end up on a wild goose chase.

However, if the vacancy is real, you might well be able to catch a client at the beginning of the process. Even though you've found a vacancy which is already known to some other recruiters, you aren't a million miles off the pace because interviews haven't begun.

What's in it for the candidate?

Similar to interview leads, the main benefit is that you will not send your candidate to companies where he has already been put forward. And, as ever, by giving you information that you can use for other candidates, he will benefit from any information you get back from them.

How can you get this information?

The exact same approach as for interview MI.

It works best if you combine the interview and application lead generation exercise into one process.

Start by asking where the candidate has had his CV sent and, after finding out, ask which companies are interviewing him.

It still works the other way around, where you start by asking about interviews and then ask whether any other companies have his CV but haven't responded yet but I've always found it flows better the first way.

WISH LIST LEADS

What are they?

Here, you need to know:

- The name of the company at which the candidate wants to work
- The location of the company
- Why the candidate wants to work there
- Whether there is any existing history or connection between the candidate and the company

Most people have a dream job but many also have a dream company.

Perhaps the office is situated close to the candidate's home. Perhaps the company operates in a particular market sector that is of great personal interest to the candidate. Perhaps he has a number of friends already working at the company. Whatever the reason, this is a company the candidate would be keen to join but, for whatever reason, he has never quite managed to get in the door.

Sometimes it's because he is afraid of rejection. Sometimes it's because he doesn't think that the company is recruiting. And sometimes it's simply because he "hasn't got around to it".

Many candidates lack the tenacity of a recruiter when it comes to accepting rejection. If somebody else is willing to pursue an application on their behalf without making the candidate do any work, it puts them in a win-win situation.

Let's do something about it and make some dreams come true.

What's in it for you?

You start with half the battle won – the candidate is already sold on the company so it is unlikely you will have to persuade him to take the interview or the job. All you need to do is convince one client that your candidate is worth interviewing and you've got a strong shot at a deal.

In short, this can be a very easy placement when it works.

What's in it for the candidate?

He gets to work at his dream company! The candidate will be grinning from ear to ear.

How can you get this information?

Straightforward – ask in as few words as possible.

"What companies would you love to work for?"

That's all you need.

When you get the answer, ask "why?"

You need to know what it is about working for that company that is so appealing to the candidate as this will help you plan your approach to the client.

If, for some strange reason, the candidate is reticent about giving you this information, remind him that you and your colleagues have an extensive network of client contacts throughout the country. There's a good chance that you will have already spoken to the relevant line manager at the company he wants to work for.

BACKFILL LEADS

What are they?

A backfill lead is when a candidate has left or is about to leave a company where his skills will continue to be needed after his exit.

You need to know:

- The name of the company the candidate has left/will be leaving
- The location of the company
- The name of the manager who is (or will soon be) one man down

What's in it for you?

If you use this information to plan the right time to approach a client, you can increase the chances that your call will be welcomed.

Bear in mind that the value of this lead varies from case to case – somebody who left a job several weeks ago may offer information about a position that has already been filled but somebody planning to hand his notice in tomorrow could lead you to a red-hot vacancy.

What's in it for the candidate?

Not much, to be honest.

If you can replace him, he might be pleased to know that his exit has not left the client in the lurch.

More materialistically, you could offer a referral fee if the candidate gives you information you then use to place business.

How can you get this information?

The straightforward method is the one mentioned above – incentivise the candidate to give you the name of his former (or soon to be former) manager by telling him that when you place business with that manager, you will pay him a referral fee. Assure the candidate that you won't tell the client where you got his name because this is something most candidates worry about. They love the referral fees but also appreciate anonymity.

The other way is to show the candidate that you are already "in" with the company. Check your database to see whether any of your colleagues have ever dealt with anybody at that company. If so, mention this to make the candidate feel comfortable that, by letting you know who his manager is, he is not opening any doors that are not already open.

A warning

When it comes to getting the name of a current client, there is another approach that will almost certainly do far more harm than good.

Saying you want the name of a candidate's boss so you can take a verbal reference is begging for trouble.

Even if you say you won't get in touch until after you've placed him, the candidate will be concerned that you might end up calling his current manager and letting slip that he could be on the way out. The candidate fears that this could undermine his negotiating power or, potentially, place his job in peril.

The only circumstance in which asking for a verbal reference from a current client might work is if the candidate has been made redundant or has already handed his notice in. In this case, his boss is already abundantly aware of the fact that his worker is leaving. If this is the case, you might get away with it.

But overall, it's not worth the risk. Once the candidate feels reluctant to give you information, regaining his trust will be hugely difficult.

CANDIDATE REFERRALS

What are they?

Most candidates know other people who work in the same field – ask them to share their contacts and you'll increase your chances of placing business.

You need:

- The name of the candidate
- How to get in touch with him
- An idea of what sort of skills he has

What's in it for you?

Asking your candidates to introduce you to other similarly skilled individuals is an excellent way of substantially increasing your resource pool.

Candidate referrals also generally guarantee quality. Providing the person referring you is a reputable candidate, he won't want to tarnish his own reputation so will only refer you to candidates he believes are talented and professional.

Even if the referred candidate isn't looking, you can start to develop your relationship so that, when he does look for a new job, he will hopefully call you first before putting his CV "out there".

This head-start gives you a chance to encourage the candidate to consider working with you exclusively. Explain the benefits of this (see the *Candidate exclusivity* chapter) and you could end up with a candidate that clients can't find through any other consultant.

What's in it for the candidate?

There are two primary benefits to the candidate offering this information – firstly, it may increase his chances of getting a job and, secondly, it may put some extra cash in his pocket via your company referral scheme (if one exists – and it should). More on that in a moment!

How can you get this information?

If you want to take the "increasing your chances" approach, point out that your client may be interested in hiring more than one person. Rather than bringing in people who don't know each other and, therefore, may not get along, if a client can hire people who already know that they can work together, he will be more confident in his decision. However, unless you are genuinely willing to market these candidates as a team or have a client who is actually interested in bringing in more than one person, this approach could lead to disappointment for the candidate in the long run.

An easier and more effective way to get what you're after is to financially incentivise the candidate. Mention that your company offers a referral fee payable *every time* you place somebody the candidate has introduced.

Keep it open!

Don't limit results by asking restrictive questions.

If you ask who your candidate knows who is looking for work, you lower your chances of getting a name.

How many of us know when our friends or colleagues are looking for work? We often don't know anything until they announce they've got a new job!

Instead, ask who the candidate recommends, irrespective of whether they are looking or not.

Explain that you would simply like to introduce yourself and see if the person in question is open to discussing a new role either now or in the future. Be sure to remind your candidate that he will get a referral fee whether you place this person in six weeks, six months or six years.

That often helps to jog minds and loosen tongues!

Why is there reluctance?

The main fear a candidate has is that the recruiter will turn into a pest who harangues his friends morning, noon and night.

If your candidate seems reticent to give you a name, point out that it is not in your interests to annoy anybody because not only will you fail to do business with the referred candidate but you will also put yourself in the original candidate's bad books.

SIGN OFF – OVERVIEW

You'd think that wrapping up a call would be an easy process and hardly something that would actually need to have its own section in a training book.

You would, however, be wrong…!

Whether it's over-talking or over-promising, there is plenty that can go wrong in the final minute of your resource call. In this section, we will look at some of the things that should (and should not) be included toward the end of your candidate calls...

SIGN OFF – INTERVIEW AVAILABILITY

It's a good idea to ask your candidate about his availability for interviews. Not only will it show him that you are serious about making progress but it will also offer an indication of how serious *he* is about his job search.

Your conversation may have led you to believe that the candidate is urgently looking for a new role. If you find out that he requires substantial notice before an interview, it suggests that his level of urgency is not perhaps as great as you might have originally thought.

- ***Don't suggest timescales*** – if you ask whether or not he would be able to make an interview with 72 hours notice (for example), you will only learn the answer to this one question.

- ***Do keep your questioning open*** – asking, "How much notice do you need before an interview?" encourages the candidate to volunteer information without you having led him in his answer.

- ***Don't accept the first answer*** – no matter what a candidate says, it is almost certain that you will be able reduce his timescales with gentle coaxing. If a candidate says he requires 72 hours before attending an interview, ask what you should do if you find a client at the end of the recruitment process who needs to interview the next day. It's your job to know!

- ***Do push until there is resistance*** – if the PAIN of his current situation is strong enough to make him a motivated jobseeker, he should make himself as available as required. Some candidates, in extreme circumstances, are willing to make excuses to their boss and "go home" early in order to attend a same day interview.

- ***Don't only ask about face-to-face interviews*** – there's no point only doing half the puzzle!

- ***Do ask about availability for telephone interviews*** – your candidate might want several hours in which to read up on the company or he may be so supremely confident in his own skills that he is willing to take a telephone interview with only a couple of minutes notice.

- ***Don't think that refusing to interview immediately indicates a lack of interest*** – maybe the candidate is still at work and can't speak freely, nor can he slip outside for a call without causing suspicion.

SIGN OFF – UPDATED CV

Even if the answer seems obvious, it's worth checking if the CV you've got is the candidate's "latest and greatest".

If you've found the CV on your company database, it could be several months – or even years – old. Just because his most recent job suggests he is working at a company "to present", that could have changed since he wrote and submitted the CV.

If you've found the CV on an online database where it looks like the candidate has recently updated it, it's likely that you have the newest version. However, there's no harm in making absolutely certain. In some cases, a candidate may have refreshed his profile but not updated his CV or, on rare occasions, mistakenly uploaded an old CV.

If you are working with a CV that isn't up-to-date, you're missing part of the puzzle. There may be items in the newest CV that make your candidate a stronger prospect. He may have worked with new technologies or gained new skills in his most recent work – if it's not on the CV you have, you won't know about it and neither will your client.

When it comes to checking, most candidates don't put a version number or a date on CVs. You'll have to read out the first line written about the most recent job, then ask whether that's the most up-to-date CV. You'll usually get a "yes" but, once in a while, you'll get "Oh, hang on – that's not it. I'd better send you through a new copy."

Most minor CV updates make no real difference but, now and then, you'll find something that turns the candidate from a decent prospect into a red-hot commodity.

SIGN OFF – CONTACT DETAILS

At the beginning of the call, you probably found the candidate's contact details on the CV – you're speaking to him right now so you've got at least one working number, right?

What if he decides to not answer his phone when you need him? What if he loses his phone or changes his number?

There are bound to be many thousands of candidates on your company database and many of them won't have been contacted for months or even years. Circumstances change and so do phone numbers. Make sure you have as many potential routes to the candidate as possible so that if one becomes unusable you have other options.

- Get a home number.
- Get a mobile number.
- Get an email address.

If you have all of these already, quickly check them. It takes seconds and the long-term benefit is huge.

SIGN OFF – SETTING EXPECTATIONS

There are many times when a recruiter can get into unintentional trouble through trying to be polite but it happens most during the sign off.

Some recruiters get into the habit of saying, "I'll call with feedback," on every resource call. Very often, the recruiter doesn't even realise that he is doing this.

You simply don't have the time to phone every single candidate back with an update. In a competitive market, it is vital for a recruiter to spend his time getting in touch with new candidates, only making callbacks to jobseekers who are progressing in the recruitment process.

Time for a reality check – the majority of people you contact about a job will not make your shortlist. Even if they do, there's no guarantee they will be selected for interview by the client.

Maybe 5% of the people you contact about a job will end up getting an interview. This means that if you give feedback to every candidate you speak to about a job, 95% of these calls will be saying, "I'm sorry, the client wasn't interested."

These calls are unnecessary for four reasons. Firstly, you learn nothing extra from them. Secondly, they take time that you could use to do something more productive (for the candidate as well as yourself!). Thirdly, they are demoralising for the candidate. And, finally, if you have to make thirty to forty of these calls every day, they will be demoralising for you as well!

A more sensible way of approaching the situation is to not set false expectations.

If you say you will call back, you can't blame a candidate for getting upset when you don't! Whilst you may think that he will forget your glib comment, he won't. Whilst he won't be waiting by the phone, he will register that you didn't live up to your word. This could create hurdles for you to overcome in the future because, now, you are seen as unreliable.

Set the correct expectation and say that you will only phone a candidate back IF the client is interested in pursuing his application. Assure him that you will do all you can but tell him not to hold his breath. This way, if the callback doesn't come, he can't be angry or disappointed with you.

It all comes down to the basic principle of under-promising and over-delivering. Unfortunately, too many recruiters over-promise and under-deliver so that's what many candidates have been conditioned to expect. Let's do something about that perception!

SIGN OFF – GET OFF THE PHONE!

Once you have got what you need from the call, wrap it up and put the phone down. Every second that you spend reiterating things you've already covered or waffling unnecessarily is a second wasted.

You might think that reaffirming the jobseeking preferences of the candidate will let him see that you have understood what has been said. Not so – this is something unconfident recruiters do to try and look more proficient or because they're not certain they've covered all of the ground required. Have faith and don't reiterate.

You don't need to go into detail about what you are going to do next – just get off the phone and do it. The candidate doesn't care about the process you will take in order to get him an interview, he just wants to know if you're going to put him forward. If so, tell him in as few words as possible and leave it at that.

Dispense with pointless politeness – I'm certainly not encouraging rudeness here but there is no need to tell a candidate to enjoy the rest of his day or to have a good weekend or any other such guff. Get out of the habit of these things as early as you can in your career. Nobody will ever refuse to deal with you because you didn't wish them a happy Friday.

Don't thank the candidate for his time. You wouldn't find a lawyer, a doctor or any other professional consultant doing this so you shouldn't do it either. Anyhow, shouldn't the candidate should be thanking *you* for *your* time? After all, he isn't paying for your service, nor will he ever. You are about to do hours of work on his behalf – so why should *you* thank *him* for giving you ten minutes of his time?

When you consider all of the above, it's easy to see how a sign off can quickly become something that takes minutes rather than seconds. If you happen to be one of the recruiters who takes 45 unnecessary seconds at the end of the call, you are wasting half an hour each day for no reason.

That's 2.5 hours each week.

Or, to put it another way, 15 full working days per year.

Is it any wonder that successful consultants finish calls by simply saying, "Okay, leave it with me," and hanging up?

POST CALL – NOTES

So, you've finished your call and now it's time to move on to the next candidate, right?

Wrong!

It is vital that you record what you have learned on your database. You might have the best memory in the entire world but there is only so much your brain can retain before the information starts leaking out of your ears! Having it safe and secure on the database will act as an excellent reminder each time you go back to speak to the candidate, allowing you to start your next conversation from a position of knowledge.

Another reason for making notes after calls is that nobody else in your company can access your brain (unless they have mad surgery skills...) but they *can* access the database. If somebody else at your company calls that same candidate only a couple of days after you and does not have access to the information you found out, he will end up covering the same ground. Not only is this a massive waste of time for your colleague and, therefore, your company but also potentially damaging to your company reputation.

Whilst your colleague is talking, the candidate will be thinking, "I've told all of this to somebody else at your company so why ask me again?" That doesn't paint a picture of a credible, professional recruitment agency.

Finally, there is the risk of absence. Let's say that you speak to a candidate, find out plenty of information but make a basic note on the system – then you fall ill and end up off work for a week. If your colleagues want to know what you found out about that candidate, they have to track you down. Rather than trying to force your fever ridden brain into recalling the nuances of a phone call from a few days ago, it's a lot easier to make a good system note as soon as you get off the phone each and every time.

Record everything

Vagueness helps nobody. If you are going to stay in control of all business situations, you need to trade on facts. Putting a comment in the notes that your candidate is finishing his contract "soon", for example, is not as helpful as a note that says he is finishing his contract on 1st April. "Soon" is open to interpretation. A concrete date is not.

The personal touch

If you learn personal information about the candidate, put this in your note as well. The fact that his children are called Jimmy and Betty might not seem highly important to you from a business perspective but it *is* very important to the candidate, so it's worth recording. The same goes for information about hobbies, likes and dislikes, anything that can lead to engagement between candidate and recruiter.

Don't waffle

You don't want your note to go on forever. Much like the call itself, you want to get as much information into as few words as possible. If you place valid points amongst huge amounts of waffle, the important things will get lost along the way.

Structure

Try and keep a standard format to your notes. This way, you will always know where to look within your note for a specific piece of information. If there is no rhyme or reason to how you lay your note out, any piece of information could be anywhere in any of your notes – that is making your job needlessly harder.

My recommendation is to structure a note as follows:

- Jobseeking motivation
- Current circumstances
- Jobseeking preferences
- Potential of counteroffer
- Leads generated
- Personal information and observations

Character observations

Don't underestimate the value of commenting on his character.

Let's say you're about to call a candidate whose previous notes suggest is a "nice guy". You'd dial the number with confidence and enter that call feeling positive.

But if you see a note suggesting the candidate has previously been judged a "tough customer", you've been warned. You might be more wary about calling but at least you aren't going in blind. You can amend your approach to something that might get you a better result.

One of my employees once found himself in this situation – five or six notes suggested he was about to speak with somebody who had previously been aggressive with other recruiters. This consultant chose to open the conversation by address the candidate as "Sir". That one word changed everything. This time, feeling that he was being spoken to with respect, the candidate was more than happy to talk and we learned more about him in that one phone call than we had learned in the previous couple of years combined.

All because of reacting to system notes.

POST CALL – FOLLOW UP

If you set the correct expectation during your resource call, you will be under no obligation to follow up. Any callback should be a business necessity.

Refining your shortlist

You might need to phone the candidate again in order to decide whether or not he will be part of a final shortlist for a vacancy. This is understandable because there is little point going into granular detail for only one job on your very first resource call. The first call is to establish the basics of the candidate's jobseeking status, motivation and preferences. Follow up calls can be to deal with specific jobs.

Checking availability

You might need to phone a candidate again because you know he was expecting feedback regarding an interview or potential extension and you want to know if he's off the market. If the candidate was offered and accepted, you can then withdraw him from any of your processes in order to keep his name "clean" with other potential clients.

Missed information

You may need to call back because you forgot something in your first call. This is fine but be aware that the more you do it, the less proficient you will seem. There isn't much harm in phoning a candidate back and saying, "Sorry, I forgot to ask you this earlier..." but doing it repeatedly suggests you need to pay more attention to getting it right first time.

Use your diary

Take any callbacks seriously. You shouldn't be setting yourself up with a mountain of follow-up work in the first place but, if there is a genuine business reason for a callback, get it in the diary – and set a reminder for yourself. Often, those who presume they will remember end up forgetting until it's too late!

CALL STRUCTURE

In order to form good habits which will help you get the most out of any candidate conversation, it's important to observe a general structure during your resource calls.

You certainly don't want to stick to a script but, at the same time, you don't want to rely on totally winging it (at least, not until you're sufficiently experienced to do so). Breaking any call down into "sections" will make your life easier and your work more effective.

My recommendation would be:

- Introduction – make it a "must take" phone call

- Jobseeking motivation – get to the bottom of the candidate's PAIN

- Current situation – understand what he'll be leaving behind

- Counteroffer – find out how likely he is to stay put

- Jobseeking preferences – understand what he wants moving forward

- Deliver and test – discuss options with the jobseeker

- Lead generation – gain information to help other candidates

Each "section" has a number of elements – those can be done in any order you fancy but sticking to a regular structure will create focus and help you get everything you need from your resourcing.

Start right now

Always discuss what the candidate is doing in his present role before you talk about what he wants in his next job. If you look to the future before you understand the present, you have no basis for comparison and, much of the time, this leads to the resourcer completely forgetting to find out anything about the current situation.

Don't dangle the carrot forever

Some recruiters prefer to do their lead generation before "rewarding" the candidate with vacancies. I'm not such a fan of that.

As you near the end of the call, the candidate is going to be itching to hear about the jobs you promised him. He's answered all of your questions very nicely, now it's time for him to get something in return. If you've done nothing but take and then attempt to take some more in the form of lead generation, he could quickly sour on you.

It's best to discuss the vacancies and then come back to lead generation. By this point (and especially if you've got some jobs the candidate wants to go for), you should have built up some trust and rapport, so your explanation as to why you need the information will be considered and, hopefully, accepted.

GHOSTS IN THE MACHINE

This is advanced stuff but worth mentioning...

Candidates who only provide a mobile number and a free email account, such as a Hotmail or Gmail, could be *anyone*.

In the majority of cases, they will be legitimate jobseekers but, on occasion, they will be phantoms – recruitment agents who have created a CV and posted it to a job board in the hopes that other agents will phone up and tell them about vacancies that the sneaky recruiter can subsequently poach.

The good news is that most recruiters simply don't have the time nor the inclination to take this underhanded approach to business and, of those who do, most of them are not convincing enough as actors to be able to fool a decent recruiter for long. Still, as a precaution, if a candidate only has a mobile number and a free email account, it is worth insisting on a home number as well. If the candidate refuses to offer this, it's a red flag. If the same candidate is also unwilling to offer verbal references from previous companies, you could be talking to one of your competitors posing as a candidate in order to try and steal your business.

Don't panic – it doesn't happen very often. But at least now you are now aware of the possibility and can therefore take adequate precautions.

UNDERSTANDING WHAT THEY DO

This will be one of the more contentious chapters and I expect some recruiters will disagree with my opinion. But it's my book, so here we go...!

You don't need to know what your candidate actually does within his job.

At least, not in huge detail.

Generally? Sure. In depth? Absolutely not.

A lot of recruiters spend a considerable amount of time on each call discussing the candidate's day-to-day duties and the skills he uses to carry out his job. Some recruiters even delve into a candidate's activity at every job listed on his CV. Whilst this may seem thorough and professional, it's actually wasting time.

If you're calling the candidate, there's a reason. He's in your call list because he has the skills that you provide to your customers (and if not, you should ask yourself why irrelevant candidates are getting into your call lists!).

By all means, get a general feel as to whether the candidate is an appropriate fit for your job but going over every element of his skillset or work history to the nth degree is creating unnecessary work.

Who's the expert?

Ask yourself this – are YOU qualified to judge the professional capabilities of the candidate?

Speaking personally, after the better part of two decades in recruitment, I believe that I am qualified to judge the aptitude of a *recruiter*.

However, I am most certainly *not* qualified to assess how suitable a technical developer or a lawyer or a plumber is to do HIS job. All I can find out is whether or not he broadly fits the brief. After that, it's the responsibility of the end client to make sure the candidate is technically capable.

Do YOUR job only

It is YOUR responsibility to find out all of the "recruitment things" about the candidate – the elements we have covered within this book such as jobseeking motivation, preferences, timescales and so forth.

If a candidate says he is an accountant and his CV strongly indicates that he is an accountant, spending 10 minutes discussing the nuances of a subject that you know little about is a gross misuse of your time.

Stick to the basic principle that if it looks like dog and barks like a dog, it's probably a dog!

URGENCY

How long should an initial candidate call take? Some people respond with, "How long is a piece of string?"

The correct response is that the call should take as long as necessary to get all the information that you need and leave your candidate feeling positive – and not a second more.

Invest your time wisely

Urgency is the business of any recruiter and you will not realise your full potential if you spend your time unwisely. Don't delude yourself that "time spent at work" is the same thing as "time spent working". If you only get six hours of productive work done in a day, you will achieve less than somebody who does eight hours of valuable work.

It is possible to do a positive, thorough and professional initial resource call – including lead generation – in around seven to ten minutes. People who say they can do it in less are likely missing major chunks of the process or not able to lead generate properly.

People who say it takes them a lot longer are either inexperienced or inefficient. Inexperience is a fair enough excuse in the early part of your career but, if you fail to improve, it will turn to inefficiency – and that is not acceptable.

LISTEN AND GUIDE

Maximise your learning from each call by minimising your talking.

When you talk, all you do is convey what you already know. When you listen, you can acquire new information.

Cast your mind back to when you were at school. For the most part, it was the teacher who did the majority of the talking. That's because he was the person you were learning from. He talked and you listened. There will have been some back-and-forth but, ultimately, you were learning from him – and you don't learn by talking.

That said, some candidates can be overly talkative. As great as it is to have a candidate who will talk freely, if he begins rambling or talking about irrelevancies, you need to politely steer him back to the point.

Imagine every phone call is like a bowling alley – the ball is the candidate and it will often not go in a straight line. You are those railings you put up for kids to stop the ball going in the gutter! When the conversation goes too far off the point, you need to guide it back to where it needs to be.

VOCAL PRESENTATION

What we say is often less important than when or how we say it.

A person who makes a valid point with zero confidence is often disbelieved or distrusted. On the other hand, some of the great speakers in history have delivered absolutely terrible statements with such conviction and credibility that people have rallied behind them unflinchingly.

Since the majority of your work is going to be on the phone, it's important you pay attention to the sound of your voice and the effect that it has on your candidates.

Pitch & tone

Sink your voice to the lowest tone that you can comfortably make and imagine that as -10. Then think about the highest tone you can manage and consider it +10. Most of the time, most people's voices will move between -5 and +5, going beyond these boundaries only when there is extreme emphasis needed.

It's the fluctuation of vocal delivery that makes speech interesting to listen to. A voice that remains in the same tone for too long is considered – and the clue is in the word – monotonous (mono tone) and boring for the listener. It creates the impression that the speaker is not a particularly dynamic individual.

If your natural voice is fairly monotonous, you're going to have to work at making your vocal presentation more interesting. However, don't overcompensate to the point that you are blatantly faking it. It's better to come across as a little dull than it is to seem phony.

Vocal subtext

Think about what the use of certain tones implies. Raising your voice to the +10 range at the end of a sentence usually implies a question. Lowering it at the end of a sentence into the -10 range implies a statement.

If you deliver a statement in the style of a question, you will confuse the listener. If you introduce yourself (a statement) but lift your voice at the end, it will sound like you are saying, "Hi, this is John Smith?"

The subtext of this is that you either do not know your own name or you are questioning if the listener knows who you are. Either way, it doesn't paint the picture of a confident, competent recruiter.

If you can combine an assured vocal delivery with excellent call content, you will have both style and substance – and that makes for a great recruiter.

VERBAL PRESENTATION

From the time we utter our first word, we are bombarded with other options to add to our vocabulary. Some of us seek out new words, try them and see what ends up sticking in our day-to-day verbiage. Others stick with the basics.

The words we use create an impression.

"Good morning! I hope the weather on this inclement day does not leave you feeling negatively disposed towards the prospect of joining me for a pleasurable stroll amongst the foliage and beneath the canopy of Mother Nature's back garden?"

Visualise the speaker of that passage. I see an English gent dressed head to toe in tweed, possibly sporting a monocle.

"Oi, weather's shit but you still up for a walk in the woods?"

What's do you see now? Tatty tracksuit? Burberry cap? Bottle of White Lightning at 10am?

And yet both people are saying the exact same thing.

Such is the beauty of words – you can paint a different picture of the same subject very easily.

"Poshing up"

Inexperienced recruiters often experiment with different verbal delivery when they are starting out, using words that would never naturally spring to their lips in an effort to seem more credible or more intelligent than they actually are. Ironically, this has the opposite effect – it makes the speaker sound like he is trying too hard. He'll sound fake or foolish (or both).

It's most evident in words such as "yourself". There is a time and place to use this word – for example, asking someone, "Were you left there by yourself?" You couldn't properly say, "Were you left there by you?" since that doesn't make sense. However, asking somebody, "Shall I send the CV through to yourself?" is attempting to "posh up" your language in order to appear intelligent. It doesn't work. In fact, it makes you seem less intelligent because it's wrong!

By all means, use complex linguistics and multi-syllable discourse but ONLY if is something that you do naturally. Very few can. Even fewer want to.

Successful consultants generally use straightforward, natural language. If a person has a natural credibility to his vocabulary, that's fine but faking it will only end up making you look like a fool.

Speech unfit for purpose

There is another side to the subject of language choices – and, in discussing this, I'm going to look like a proper grumpy old man but it's something we've got to cover.

You have to speak in a manner which is fit for purpose. A bling-encrusted rapper can get away with paying no attention to grammatical accuracy (and is prob'ly encouraged to frow out his fissoorus) but that's not acceptable for a recruiter. You wouldn't have any faith in a lawyer, a doctor or an accountant if he couldn't handle the basics of his own first language so, if you want to be a successful recruiter, present yourself in the same light as these other professionals.

As tough as it might be, consider whether you do any of the following – and, if so, correct them:

• *Using the wrong person*

By this, I mean saying things like "We was going" rather than "We were going" or, "What was you doing?" instead of "What were you doing?"

• *Using the wrong tense*

Some people choose to go with "I done" instead of "I did" or "I seen" rather "I saw". Don't be one of them!

• *Mispronunciation*

Settle in – this one's a particular bugbear of mine since I live in England and we've become pretty ropey as a nation when it comes to elements of our own language...

I'm not talking about simple snafus or regional dialects, I'm on about mispronouncing letters to the point where it changes the meaning of the word you're saying.

The most common example of this in Britain is known as TH fronting – making the "F" noise in a word that calls for "TH". It is most often seen in people who start counting by saying "one, two, free, four, five…"

Most listeners will know what you mean because of the context in which you say it but why should the speaker expect the listener to decipher what is meant? Let's be honest, we would raise more than an eyebrow if somebody counted "one, two, three, thour, thive..."

This "speech defect" actually changes the meaning of the word. Three is a number. Free means no cost.

It is similar in other cases – for example, "thrills" are what you get from going on a rollercoaster. "Frills" are what you put on a party dress. They are entirely different things. Don't get me started on "thought" vs. "fought"!

If you do it, don't beat yourself up – it's likely not your fault. Do your parents do it? Did your teachers? Or have you been weaned on a steady televisual diet of The Only Way Is Essex and other such intellectual treats? It's become so prevalent in the UK since the millennium especially that you won't go a day without hearing it. A lot.

But in most cases it's not a speech *defect*. People *can* correct it, they just don't.

Here's the technical explanation.

The "F" noise is easier to make than the "TH" noise. As a child, the "F" noise will come more quickly into our grasp than the "TH" noise and so, when trying to replicate the words that we hear that start with "TH", we do our best impression but substitute an "F" at the beginning. That's how it begins. It doesn't help that when a kid loses his front teeth, he is deprived of the ability to make this noise for a while!

Some parents and teachers will help the child learn how to make the "TH" noise correctly. Other parents and teachers will say "close enough" and leave it there. If the parents also mispronounce "F" for "TH" themselves, the kid will grow up thinking (or "finking") that this is genuinely how certain words are said. But this doesn't mean that the kid *can't* make the "TH" sound – he just hasn't trained himself to do so yet.

To break this habit after years and years is difficult but not impossible. It just takes time, effort and – most of all – the want to sound as credible as possible.

There's also the dropping of Ts and Gs in words (so that "getting" becomes "geh-in") by the Brits whilst Americans often transform T into D ("getting" becomes "gedding") but at least these don't change the meaning of words entirely!

Dog words/phrases

We've all got them.

Irrelevant utterances that creep into sentences when we have nothing else to say. Things that pad out our speech and indicate that we are either uncertain of our point or unconfident in our delivery.

Words that add nothing to the sentence. "Basically". "Obviously". "Clearly".

Nothing constructions that have become catchphrases – "you know?"

And let's not forget the 21st century's most prevalent dog word – "like". A word that should be used to mean "similar to" or to express enjoyment of something, yet like people under the age of like thirty seem to like feel compelled to throw it in to each like sentence like three or four times. Like.

There's a time and a place for it. "I like cake." There you are – logical and factual. But, "I was like talking to the client and he was like 'ok, find somebody' and I'm like sure, I'll do what I can..." makes you sound like you're the talky bit in the middle of a Taylor Swift song rather than a professional like consultant.

And then you have the classic "um" and "err" and "uh" that punctuate many peoples' conversation. Very few of us are free of these things – even now as I approach forty, I still catch myself saying "um" more than I would like. However, you *can* get these tics under control by paying attention to your verbal delivery and working actively to improve it.

Diminutives

Using the words "just", "only" or "quick" in relation to your call is not productive (unless it genuinely is a quick call which will only last seconds!).

A lot of people have the habit of starting a phone call by saying that "it's only a quick call". This sets the wrong expectation because if this is the first time you have ever spoken to a candidate, it's unlikely that it is *actually* going to be a quick call.

It also undermines the importance of the call before it has even started. If you are going to make the phone call seem inconsequential before it has even got started, why on earth should the candidate give you his time?

It's not "just a quick call"– it's the most important call the candidate is going to receive today! If you don't believe this, why should he?

And why should he give you his precious time?

"Sort of" and "kind of" fall into this category too. Is what you are offering your candidate "sort of a good vacancy" or "a good vacancy"?

Swearing

I don't care if your client does it. You don't.

He may not hear it when *he* slides a casual "shit" into the conversation but you'd better believe he'll notice if *you* do!

Negatives

This is a bizarre affliction of the British that doesn't seem to affect Americans. When asked, "How are you?", altogether too many Brits reply with, "Not bad."

Firstly, it doesn't actually answer the question. You're being asked how you *are*, not how you are *not*!

Secondly, why present your reply in a negative fashion? "Not" is a negative word. "Bad" is a negative word. Say them too many times and you subconsciously fill a conversation with negativity. That's the last thing you want when trying to get candidate and client to say "YES!"

It's the same for "no worries", "not a problem" and any other such phrases. Be proactively positive! Get words like "great", "fantastic" and "excellent" into your conversations and everybody will come away from the call feeling upbeat.

Overstatements

The Great Wall of China. The Taj Mahal. The Pyramids. The Coliseum. Those are all awesome. They inspire awe.

Your lunch may be very nice but it's probably not quite in the same category.

The same goes for epic. I'm sure everybody involved in creating such cinematic epics as Lawrence of Arabia, Gone with the Wind, Titanic, Gladiator and the Lord of the Rings films would be less than thrilled to hear your Friday night pint of beer is also "epic".

Colloquialism or slang

There's a time and place for slang and it's not on an initial resource call.

Once you've placed your candidate and know him well, perhaps you can get away with calling him "mate" but don't undermine yourself by dropping the M-bomb in your first call.

The same goes for "pal", "fella", "geezer" and any other cheeky chappery. Leave it to the cockneys – it's got no place in business.

The same goes for US terms of overfamiliarity - I'm certain few clients enjoy being called "buddy".

Fifties remnant "cool" still finds its way into too many professional conversations. If a lawyer wouldn't use it in court, you shouldn't be using it on the phone. The same goes for anything else that might cause a client to think you're still at school and desperately courting the approval of your peers – "sick", "swag", "ratchet", "totes amaze" – any of this crap wouldn't be used by any self-respecting professional. Well, except for maybe the sentence "that terrible rookie recruiter kept saying 'swag' and 'totes amaze' and it made me so sick, I hit him with a ratchet". And I guess doctors and the dude from Big Hero 6 can get away with "sick". But that's it.

Parroting

Candidate:	"I'm looking for a new job"
You:	"You're looking for a new job. How far are you willing to commute?"
Candidate:	"About half an hour"
You:	"About half an hour. How do you feel about contract work?"
Candidate:	"I'm not really that keen"
You:	"You're not really that keen"
Candidate:	"Hold on, is there an echo in here?"
You:	"Hold on, is there an echo in here?"
Candidate:	"That's really annoying, stop it"
You:	"That's really annoying, stop it"

It's like a comedy sketch written by a six year old. Don't get involved!

Why do these things happen?!

You could probably trace several of these issues to not being corrected or encouraged by your parents. You could blame TV. You could say that the education system failed you.

Those are all excuses. As the saying goes, when you point a finger, three fingers point right back at you.

If you're aware that the above examples are not the best way of using the English language, yet you are doing nothing to improve your own delivery, you're your own worst enemy. If you were previously unaware of any of these points, now you know and can do something about them.

And you absolutely *should* do something about them – some candidates may not care how you speak but some will silently judge you as less capable or less intelligent if you cannot present yourself professionally.

A candidate or client will *never* shy away from dealing with you because you speak *properly*.

They *may* have reservations about you if you don't.

QUESTIONING

A lot of resourcers ask a lot of questions. That's a good start. However, if you ask the *wrong* questions, you waste everybody's time.

We've been through what you need to learn from a candidate call so, by now, you should have an idea of *what* questions you need to ask.

This chapter is about *how* to ask those questions.

And the simplest answer is "using as few words as possible".

When you ask a question by using limited words, there is little room for misinterpretation. Add unnecessary words into your question and the candidate may get confused about what it is you want to know.

Open Questions

Of the many thousands in the English language, great resourcing boils down to six words...

- Who?
- What?

- When?
- Where?
- Why?
- How?

When your sentences begin with these words, you will find out a lot about the person you are speaking to. Whilst a closed question offers only options (usually "yes" or "no"), an open question turns the conversation over to the candidate and encourages him to respond openly.

Think about this – you start a call by asking a candidate if he is looking for work. Closed question.

If the candidate says "yes", you could then ask him, "Is it because you want more money?"

No.

"Is it because you don't like your current commute?"

No.

"Is it because you are not happy with how your career is progressing?"

No.

This could go on for quite some time – it's like a game of Guess Who, whittling away the options that it *isn't* until you finally figure out what it *is*.

A simpler method is to ask "Why are you looking for a new job?"

Eight words.

Eight words and now the candidate will use many multiples of eight words in order to tell you exactly what his PAIN is.

If you give the candidate an option to which he can simply say "yes", you may find the answer but won't understand his reasons.

Multiple choice

A common habit amongst recruiters is asking an open question and then immediately offering the candidate multiple choice answers.

This is either down to a lack of confidence on the part of the recruiter (he's afraid the candidate won't answer) or because the recruiter wants to show that he is so clever that he can correctly answer questions for other people.

When we offer multiple choice answers, we presume to know what the candidate thinks – and this is often tarred by our own (often flawed) view of the world. It's especially common in younger recruiters who don't yet appreciate that somebody in his late thirties or early forties has a different perspective on life to somebody fresh out of school or University.

Inferred open questions

Sticking the word "or" at the end of your sentence and trailing off isn't the same as asking an open question.

"Are you happy to commute half an hour or...?"

It looks stupid on paper. It also sounds stupid when delivered but it often slips under the radar.

"Are you happy to commute half an hour?" is a closed question. YES/NO. Choose one.

"Are you happy to commute half an hour or...?"

Where's the rest of that sentence?!

It's the "other" box on a questionnaire. Fill it in yourself, Mr. Candidate. Complete my thought because I don't know what the rest of it is. If I'm wrong with the half an hour thing, please clue me in. It's sort of open but also sort of vague. A good recruiter doesn't like vagueness.

Double questions

Another stumbling block is asking more than one question at a time.

Fearing that his first question wasn't clear, an inexperienced recruiter may rephrase and redeliver. Worse still, sometimes he'll follow up an excellent question with a different question about a different subject. Sometimes, both get answered. Other times, only one does.

Have confidence. Ask one question in as few words as possible, hush up and listen.

Listening to talking ratio

A simple way of figuring out if you are using enough open questions is to consider who is doing the majority of the talking. If you find yourself speaking for a solid eight minutes of a ten minute phone call, you are getting this wrong. As mentioned before, you learn by listening – so the candidate should be doing the majority of the talking in response to your concise, relevant questions.

ENGAGEMENT

Every phone call offers the opportunity to engage with a candidate on a personal level.

Recruitment is about relationships – and it is tough to have a relationship if you know little about what makes the other party tick. I'm not saying that you should spend five minutes on every call delving into the deepest personal secrets of the jobseeker but there is value in taking a glimpse at the "person behind the worker" – and, in turn, giving him a glimpse of the "person behind the recruiter".

On the CV...

Some candidates have an "interests" section on their CV. If you notice something in which you and the candidate share an interest, it could act as common ground. Whether it's football, golf, cookery, crocheting, disco dancing, caber tossing or playing strip poker, the fact that you have an interest in common with the candidate will help him warm to you more quickly.

It also has the benefit of helping you stand out from all the other recruiters who will be speaking to him. Rather than being "just another recruiter", you will be the "golf recruiter" or the "disco recruiter" – a small differentiation but an important one nonetheless!

People like people like them

If a candidate finds himself choosing between two comparable offers, what he thinks of the recruiter can actually make the difference.

A candidate is more likely to accept the job presented by a recruiter he likes and trusts because, firstly, it is harder to let down a friend than an acquaintance and, secondly, he knows that he can trust you to do your best for him if he has any issues with the job.

Building rapport with a candidate can also help with lead generation. Once he understands that you won't use any anything he says to his detriment, he will be more likely to offer you market information.

Understanding the likes and dislikes of your candidate can give you an edge when it comes to creating the right shortlist for your client. If you know that your client is a football fan and you can't decide who to put forward out of two similarly qualified candidates, finding out that one of them loves football and the other absolutely detests it will allow you to place your bet on the right horse.

Not on the CV...

If there is no indication of the candidate's interests in his CV, you'll have to take another approach.

Listen for opportunity during your conversation – a lot of candidates will speak about their family, for example. If you pick up on this, you can find out what his partner does or how many children he has. These might not seem particularly useful facts to you but, to the candidate, these are major parts of his life. Get the candidate talking about them and he will go on for ages.

If you've had a friendly call, consider wrapping up by enquiring if he's got any plans for the weekend or an upcoming break. It's another chance to learn a little more about what the candidate is like as a person rather than just as "talent".

Be an interestED, interestING person...

Showing an interest in other people and what they care about is half the battle won – the other half is giving something back about yourself. Being interesting makes you memorable – and that's key to being a top recruiter.

What is interesting about you? If your answer is "nothing", you either need to stop being so modest or get off your backside and find a hobby! Once you've found something memorable about yourself, the challenge is to work it into conversation so it can help you stand out from your competitors.

Of course, you can't just blurt out, "I'm a black belt in karate..." and hope for the best – you've got to build up to that declaration.

You could get there by different routes. If you're talking to a candidate about his time at school/university, you could find out which sports he played and make the link that way. If you find out that he has a child, that could lead to asking about what sort of things the kid is into before then divulging that you yourself were heavily into karate as a child... and kept it up all the way through to the highest grade.

You can do this with anything – don't just TAKE. You've got to build the opportunity to GIVE.

If you know somebody who works in the same industry as the candidate's partner, tell him! If he is talking about his kids, speak of your experience with children. If you aren't a parent, perhaps you are an uncle or aunt. Maybe you have friends with kids – use anything that can help show your candidate that you are a "real person" too!

Give the candidate the chance to get to know you and you never know – he might like you. And even though "like" isn't quite as important in business as "respect", they're both powerful emotions – and somebody who can combine the two will go a long way.

CANDIDATE EXCLUSIVITY

It's rare to find a candidate who is willing to leave his job search in the hands of just one recruiter but it's definitely worth discussing, since such an arrangement can seriously benefit both sides.

What do you need?

You want the candidate to deactivate his profile on any online CV database and tell any other recruiter who approaches him that he is off the market.

What's in it for you?

A candidate jobseeking exclusively through you means that you don't have to worry about other agencies applying pressure to close the candidate down before anybody else can.

You also gain the ability to tell prospective clients the only way they can engage the candidate is through you – and if the talent is talented enough, it's a great door opener.

What's in it for him?

The candidate now doesn't have to contend with numerous agents badgering him to accept the first offer he is made. By working solely with a single agent who he likes and respects, he can make a reasoned decision about what is best for him without undue pressure from multiple third parties.

Also, by committing to you, he puts himself at the top of your hotlist and becomes somebody you are more likely to actively market than another candidate who is on the books of numerous agencies.

Who should you target?

Candidates you have placed before have seen what you are capable of so are more likely to believe in you and agree to exclusivity. However, that's not to say you can't convince people you've never worked with before to go for it. All you can do is sell the benefits and see what they think.

Pitfalls

It's tough to convince a candidate to trust you so much that he relies on you and only you for his next job – and it's tough to have that pressure on your shoulders. Only accept it if you feel confident you can guarantee him a placement.

It's also worth being aware of the fact that, even if the candidate says he will work with you exclusively, he may already have his details with other agencies. Even if he's not actively working with them, they may phone up and offer him an incredible opportunity – and he's under no legal obligation to turn them down.

LEAVING MESSAGES

You've prepped, you've called and there's no answer.

So, to leave a message or to not leave a message? That, Mr. Shakespeare, is *actually* the question.

Well, if you don't leave a message, the candidate doesn't know who to come back to, when and why. At least if you leave a message, there's a chance he'll call you back.

If, of course, you've already left a message recently, leaving a second (or third, fourth, fifth...) might seem desperate so avoid these unless it's absolutely vital.

There are a couple of different schools of thought when it comes to leaving messages for candidates.

- Leave as much information as possible
- Leave as little information as possible

I prefer the second approach.

When it comes to getting a candidate to call you back, giving him stacks of information about your tremendously exciting job, the location, the money and the prospects may well inspire him to pick up the phone and get in touch but if *any* part of the job doesn't appeal, he will say "not interested".

The problem is that he won't say this *to you*. He'll say it in his head, delete the message and carry on with his life. And, because he doesn't call you back, you learn nothing.

A "bare minimum" message can cause a candidate to call back out of sheer curiosity.

Saying, "I've got an excellent job opportunity which I think will really suit you…" and nothing else will give the candidate very little he can disagree with so the likelihood is that he *will* phone you back to find out more.

If it turns out that the job in question is not for him, you can at least find out why. This will then either give you something to work with (e.g. he likes the job but thinks the money is too low – so you can see if the client would be interested in this candidate at a higher rate/salary) or it will give you an insight into the jobseeking preferences of the candidate which you can then apply to future resourcing.

Get it on the system!

Even if you only leave a message, you still need to register the activity on your company database. Some might say this is a waste of time because nothing was learned but, in fact, you did learn something. You learned that this candidate did not answer his phone at this particular time on this particular day.

If other people have registered similar notes in the past, you start to see a pattern and it becomes clear that anybody who phones this candidate at a specific time or on a specific day will likely get the same result. This will then allow future callers to make a better judgement on their approach to this candidate.

Another reason to note that you have left a message is that, unless you do, nobody else in your company will know. If the candidate calls back but didn't catch your name on the message, the note on the database will allow anybody in the company to see who called him.

Also, if somebody else from the company is about to phone this candidate and can see that you have recently left a message, he might think twice about leaving another. We don't want multiple people from the same company leaving multiple messages for the same candidate on the same day – this creates the impression that the company is disorganised, pushy and unprofessional.

Finally, if you learned anything about the candidate from his CV whilst the phone was ringing, jot it down in your "left message" note. This way, the information you have found will leap to your attention the next time you (or anybody else) next tries to contact him. You may not have managed to get through today but, at the very least, the time you spent looking at his CV will have some lasting value.

THE WRITTEN WORD

Fittingly enough, the final words in this book are going to be about words themselves.

You've just read about 25,000 of them and, unless my proofing skills are letting me down, I'd hope there are no mistakes. Mistakes undermine the credibility of the writer (I've set myself up for a fall there!).

Just imagine if I quickly typed up some thoughts on my computer, didn't bother re-reading it and published what is supposed to be a professional piece of writing by an expert in his field.

I'll d luk lik an nidiot.

Of course, it's pretty unlikely that you'll ever have to write 25,000 words for *your* job but those you *do* write still have to be fit for purpose. Remember – they are part of your professional presentation. You wouldn't expect substandard syntax and shoddy spelling from a doctor, accountant, solicitor... if you want to be in the same league, make sure you're not undermining yourself on paper.

You don't need to be able to spin a Shakespearean sonnet, paint with poetry like Poe, engage and enchant like Rowling or grapple with grammar like Foley (an odd collection of writing references for sure!). You simply need to be able to string a few sentences together in a manner that does not make you look like you skipped most of your English lessons.

Here are a few errors that can turn a recruiter from dude to dud in the reader's eyes...

Right spelling, wrong word

This comes from overreliance on spell-check. If technology is doing the brain work for you, you're asking it to understand the point you are trying to make and that's a step too far, even for the smartest of smartphones. Observe the ongoing stream of hilarious and highly embarrassing auto-text fails that seep through the world of social media on a daily basis.

A clergyman scheduled to officiate a wedding might write that he is off to church to unite a young couple. That's wonderful – as long as he spells the words correctly. A slip of the fingers and "unite" becomes "untie" and then the reader will wonder why this priest has a young couple tied up in his church in the first place. Spell-check won't save him since he hasn't made a *spelling* mistake.

Somebody who is a "bare man" is wearing nothing. Somebody who is a "bear man" is half-man, half-bear (or has a disturbing fetish we don't need to discuss...)

In a similar vein, a police report stating a shop-owner was "robbed" is different to one stating that a shop-owner was "robed". One had a gun pointed at his head and money whipped from the till, the other was wearing a dressing gown. Only one extra letter but a world of difference!

Brought/Bought

"I brought these grapes from the shop" – the person in question has physically moved the grapes from the shop to wherever he is now.

"I bought these grapes from the shop" – the person in question has used money to purchase the grapes.

Use the right word for the right purpose!

They're/their/there

"They're over there with their friends"

That's a vague but grammatically correct sentence.

"There over their with they're friends", on the other hand, is absolute dribble.

- "They're" – they are
- "Their" = belonging to them
- "There" = generally positional ("the lemon is over there"), occasionally used in fairytales ("There once was a beautiful Princess...")

We're/Were/Where

- "We're" = abbreviated present tense of the verb "to be" (e.g. we are at the party)

- "Were" = past tense of the verb "to be" (e.g. "we were at the party")
- "Where" = positional ("the place where the party is happening")

Could have/Could of

When people get this one wrong, it's the visual equivalent of sharp nails on a blackboard.

The reason some people write "could of" is because, when spoken, "could have" is sometimes contracted to "could've", much like "it is" becomes "it's" – eliminate one of the sounds, speak faster, all good.

Except for when it ends up going wrong.

The issue is that "could've" sounds like "could of" more than "could have", so some people end up writing "could of".

You'd hope that parents, teachers, bosses and so forth would have picked up on this and done something about it but apparently some people either never get guidance (or ignore what they're told).

And so we end up with "could of" – which MAKES NO SENSE IN ENGLISH.

Whenever I see this in an email, I roll my eyes and shake my head.

Is that the reaction you want to inspire in candidates?

Faking it

In the same way that some people speak in a different manner when they're attempting to seem professional, others present themselves on paper in the style they believe will give them extra credibility as a highly articulate and incredibly intelligent individual.

And it usually makes the writer look like a total tool.

If you received an email which began, *"Pertaining to the recent discourse held on the penultimate Friday of last month, I now find myself in a position to postulate a theorem as to why the canine performed a bowel movement in the salon..."* you'd be baffled to say the least. Either the Victorians have figured out time travel (and email!) or the person emailing you is trying to look ever so clever.

Be genuine – keep it simple. People can spot a phony a mile off and they'd much rather get an email saying, "After our chat the other week, I think I know why the dog took a dump in the living room" (although I guess it depends on whose living room we're talking about).

Slumming it

On the other side of the writing quality coin, don't be so casual about it that you lapse into slang, laziness or, worst of all, txt spk. By all means, text away to your mates on your phone but leave it out when it comes to your professional presentation.

Another issue that people unexpectedly encounter is a lack of capital letters. If you're going to write, write right! "I" when referring to yourself is *always* capitalised. The first word in a sentence is *always* capitalised. Names are *always* capitalised.

Dropping capital letters can change the meaning of words. Midway through a sentence, "Reading" is a place whereas "reading" is what you're doing right now with this book. "Bath" is a place in Southern England and "bath" is a place to relax, unwind and possibly do some reading. Not Reading.

Just like the listener can usually figure out what the speaker means because of the context, the reader can usually work out what the writer is trying to say – but that's not the reader's job. It's yours.

If you're lazy on paper/email, it suggests that you have a similar attitude towards your work. You've got enough hurdles to overcome in your job without creating more through lack of effort in your professional presentation.

Don't negotiate by email

Negotiation is to be done by phone, never by email. On the phone, you can hear the vocal reaction of the other person.

A person can say "fine" with inflection that makes it mean, "Yes, this is actually fine..." or, "No, this is not actually fine but I'm going to go along with it unhappily."

By email, "fine" is "fine". You don't get to know how the word was delivered so you can't interpret how "fine" the candidate actually is with your proposal.

Another issue caused by email negotiation is that you can't control the reaction. If you are on the phone and propose something that the candidate does not like, you can find out what the issue is then and there and have a discussion about it. If you propose something unpalatable by email, the candidate may simply ignore it and walk away – and you've lost control of the situation.

By all means, market by email. Introduce yourself by email. Share information by email. But when it comes to areas that require you to carefully listen to how the candidate is presenting himself vocally and verbally, do it in person or on the phone.

Wrapping up

Like ending a phone call, there's no need to spend your time recapping or observing lengthy pleasantries – that's wasting time for both you and the candidate.

Email is a less formal method of communication than letter writing, so there's no need to finish on "Yours sincerely" or "Faithfully" or "I have the honour of being..." per the quills and ink era.

Don't overthink it – choose something you like and roll with it, whether it's "Best regards", "Best", "Kind regards", "Yours" – pick what works best for you and don't drag it out. Get it wrapped up and move on.

Speaking of which...

All the best,
Ross
rw@therecruitmentor.com

Other titles in The RecruitMentor series

The RecruitMentor – Client calls

The RecruitMentor – Vacancy qualification and the placement process

For more information, visit

www.therecruitmentor.com

Lightning Source UK Ltd.
Milton Keynes UK
UKOW06f1329290316

271094UK00002B/2/P